A Visa for a Dream

THE NEW IMMIGRANTS SERIES

Allyn & Bacon

Series Editor, Nancy Foner, State University of New York at Purchase

Changing Identities: Vietnamese Americans, 1975-1995, by James M. Freeman

From the Workers' State to the Golden State: Jews from the Former Soviet Union in California, by Steven J. Gold

From the Ganges to the Hudson: Indian Immigrants in New York City, by Johanna Lessinger

Salvadorans in Suburbia: Symbiosis and Conflict, by Sarah J. Mahler

A Visa for A Dream: Dominicans in the United States, by Patricia R. Pessar

A Visa for a Dream:
Dominicans in the United States

Patricia R. Pessar
Yale University

Allyn and Bacon
Boston • London • Toronto • Sydney • Tokyo • Singapore

To my grandmothers,
Lee Oberfield and Eva Pessar

Contents

Foreword to the Series

The United States is now experiencing the largest wave of immigration in the country's history. The 1990s, it is predicted, will see more new immigrants enter the United States than in any decade in American history. New immigrants from Asia, Latin America, and the Caribbean are changing the American ethnic landscape.

Until recently, immigration was associated in the minds of many Americans with the massive influx of southern and eastern Europeans at the turn of the century. Since the late 1960s, America has again become a country of large-scale immigration, this time attracting newcomers from developing societies of the world. The number of foreign-born is at an all-time high: nearly 20 million foreign-born persons were counted in the 1990 census. Although immigrants are a smaller share of the nation's population than they were earlier in the century—8 percent in 1990 compared to about 15 percent in 1910—recent immigrants are having an especially dramatic impact because their geographic concentration is greater today. About half of all immigrants entering the United States during the 1980s moved to eight urban areas: Los Angeles, New York, Miami, Anaheim, Chicago, Washington, D.C., Houston, and San Francisco. America's major urban centers are, increasingly, immigrant cities with new ethnic mixes.

Who are the new immigrants? What are their lives like here? How are they redefining themselves and their cultures? And how are they contributing to a new and changing America? The *New Immigrants Series* provides a set of case studies that explores these themes among a variety of groups. Each book in the series is written by a recognized expert who has done extensive in-depth ethnographic research on one of the immigrant groups. The groups represent a broad range of today's arrivals, coming from a variety of countries and cultures. The studies cover a wide geographical range as well, based on research done in different parts of the country, from New York to California.

Most of the books in the series are written by anthropologists. All draw on qualitative research that shows what it means to be an immigrant in America today. As part of each study, individual immigrants tell their stories, which will help give a sense of the experiences and problems of the newcomers. Through the case studies, a dynamic picture emerges of the way immigrants are carving out new lives for themselves at the same time as they are creating a new and more diverse America.

The ethnographic case study, long the anthropologist's trademark, provides a depth often lacking in research on immigrants in the United States. Many anthropologists, moreover, like a number of authors in the *New Immigrants Series*, have done research in the sending society as well as in the United States. Having field experience at both ends of the migration chain makes anthropologists particularly sensitive to the role of transnational ties that link immigrants to their home societies. With first-hand experience of immigrants in their home culture, anthropologists are also well positioned to appreciate continuities as well as changes in the immigrant setting.

As the United States faces a growing backlash against immigration, and many Americans express ambivalence and sometimes hostility toward the latest arrivals, it becomes more important than ever to learn about the new immigrants and to hear their voices. The case studies in the *New Immigrants Series* will help readers understand the cultures and lives of the newest Americans and bring out the complex ways the newcomers are coming to terms with and creatively adapting to life in a new land.

NANCY FONER
Series Editor

Acknowledgments

My greatest debt is to the many Dominicans in New York and on the island who shared their lives and histories with me. At first most had understandable doubts about my purposes. For had their suspicions been justified, our conversations might have led to the deportation of one informant who shared his undocumented status with me, or the termination of benefits for another who confided that she stretched inadequate welfare payments with off-the-books wages. In an attempt to diminish such fear, I promised my informants anonymity. Yet, the practice of providing anonymity is double-edged. While the reader has the pleasure of hearing the informants' voices resounding throughout the text, I am regretably not at liberty to share their names with my readers or personally thank them for all their support and help. So I am forced to fall back on the popular cliché and say to all with much gratitude, "You know who you are."

A spirit of great collegiality prevails among many of the students of Dominican migration. I want to thank Lourdes Bueno, Max Castro, Jorge Duany, Eugenia Georges, Greta Gilbertson, Anneris Goris-Rosario, Pamela Graham, Sherri Grasmuck, Luis Guarnizo, Douglas Gurak, Daisann McLane, and Silvio Torres-Saillant for generously sharing their research with me. For helping to enrich my understanding of the Dominican diaspora, I express my gratitude to Sakinah Carter, Ana Jiménez-Bautista, Victor Mejía, Radame Rodríguez, and María Villarreal. My research was also greatly facilitated by the assistance of colleagues at the City University's Dominican Studies Institute.

Greta Gilbertson and Silvio Torres-Saillant also kindly agreed to read an earlier draft of the book and their comments proved invaluable. Nancy Foner, a long-time friend and supportive colleage, deserves special thanks for inviting me to participate in the series on New Immigrants and for guiding the manuscript, with the help of Sylvia Shepard, through two drafts.

My four-year-old son, Matthew, deserves praise for his ability to function happily and creatively as the son of academic parents. During many of my seemingly interminable stints at the word processor, Matthew kept himself entertained by peering over my shoulder and counting the number of words that began with his favorite letter, "M." I reserve my final expression of gratitude for my husband, Gil Joseph, whose championing spirit and tremendous generosity led him to patiently read and edit every page of this book, pose the really tough questions, and demand the best from me.

Introduction

Dominicans are one of the fastest growing immigrant populations in the United States. Like all recent immigrants, Dominicans have clustered in only a few states, with New York far in the lead. In fact today, Dominicans are the single largest immigrant group residing in New York. This book is about these Dominican New Yorkers.

If the average American knows anything about Dominicans in the United States, it may well be through media coverage of famous Dominican, major league baseball players like Juan Marachal, George Bell, Pedro Guerrero, or Sammy Sosa or the sensational depiction of Dominicans in the New York media as a population heavily involved in the drug trade. The Dominicans portrayed in the media, however, are not representative of this immigrant group. As a young Dominican film maker states:

> I grew up here, in Washington Heights... I've seen how they bust their butts, trying to provide for their families. I've seen how they pour money into the New York economy. But for most people Dominicans are only known for two things: selling drugs and playing baseball....What about the working people; the young people trying to get an education and struggling to pay for it?" ("Up From the Heights," Educational Video Center).

When not stereotyped as baseball players and drug dealers, Dominicans are frequently portrayed as an undifferentiated mass—"The Dominicans." Of course Americans tend to speak in such global, homogenous terms about most racial and ethnic populations in the United States. In this study I hope to avoid sweeping generalizations about a fiction called "The Dominicans." Rather, I will try to provide an appreciation of the differences as well as the commonalities that characterize members of this ethnic group. I will describe people who fled the Dominican Republic for political reasons, as well as others who left in search of economic mobility. There are some who have done extremely well, either attaining the "American Immigrant Dream" of going from "rags to riches," or enjoying the "Dominican Dream" of returning home with the accoutrements of an upper-class lifestyle. There are also many, indeed the majority of Dominican New Yorkers, who are less successful and for whom both dreams remain elusive.[1] For them, the challenge is to build a supportive and empowering ethnic community in New York to help in their struggles with a deteriorating New York economy, poverty, and racial and ethnic discrimination.

Authors of books about foreign and ethnic populations, like Dominicans, have increasingly been accused of "orientalism"—turning people who are "different" into exotic "others." In this study, I have tried to follow the advice of a Dominican colleague who cautioned me to avoid both essentialism and exoticism. Dominican New Yorkers, he told me "are as ugly and as beautiful, as good, and as evil as everyone else" (Silvio Torres-Saillant, personal communication 1995).

In chapter one, we will see that like European immigrants of an earlier era, Dominicans confront hardships in their country of origin and come to the United States in search of a better life. They rely extensively on their immediate and extended families to sponsor their outmigration and to help in resettlement abroad. Indeed, Dominican immigration is very much about the building and maintenance of social networks of kin and friends—networks that often encompass both New York and communities in the Dominican Republic. Chapter two's discussion of Dominican settlement in New York City brings out the crucial role of social networks in guiding newcomers to key destinations, such as Washington Heights, the heart of the Dominican community in New York. What becomes clear is that Dominicans have both placed their mark upon, and accommodated to, the lifeways and institutions encountered in New York City.

When Dominican New Yorkers speak among themselves or with others about their migration experiences, certain phrases are likely to recur. "No había futuro" ("There was no future"), they explain, to justify why they left a beloved homeland. Not surprisingly, they go on to say that they have come to the United States "buscando mejor vida" ("in search of a better life") and to *"progresar"* ("to advance economically"). At first glance, there would appear to be a baffling inconsistency between these aspirations and the choice of New York City as the economic mecca. Chapter three explores why, despite its overall economic decline, New York City continues to afford job opportunities to many new immigrants, such as Dominicans. It also examines how different segments of the Dominican New Yorker population have fared both socially and economically over the last few decades.

In Chapter four I turn to a discussion of Dominican families in New York, a topic which highlights, in a dramatic way, both continuities and changes in the lives of Dominican New Yorkers as a consequence of immigration. Although I concentrate on the impact of women's waged-employment for gender relations in Dominican families, I also consider how children's new roles as cultural brokers have affected generational hierarchies.

Although many native-born Americans assume that immigrants come to settle permanently, this is not what many immigrants have in mind. Many Dominicans intend to return home in order to best enjoy and validate their hard-fought gains in social and economic standing. In their words, in New York, "hay trabajo pero no hay vida" ("There is work, but there is no life"). Although the majority never do make it home again, most retain strong social, cultural, and economic ties to the island republic—an accomplishment that at the very least makes a return possible. In the final chapter, I explore why and how many Dominicans have attempted to forge binational lives "aquí" ("here," in the United States) and "allá" ("there," in the Dominican Republic). Some critics of immigration argue that this transnational stance does not permit new immigrants and ethnics to fully integrate into U.S. society and culture. This critique overlooks the common perception and experience of many immigrants and ethnics who feel that they are not, and may never be, welcomed as full participants in this country. The critique also overlooks counter-evidence which shows that Dominican New Yorkers' links and loyalties to both U.S. and Dominican society can be complementary and mutually reinforcing, rather than contradictory and opposed. We are speaking of truly transnational people who refuse to choose between two societies, particularly when both provide them with valued identities, social relations, and resources.

RESEARCH METHODS

As an ethnographer I have gained insight into the Dominican population by speaking over time to many people, at great length, about their own lives, their families, their friends, and their communities. Ethnography, and the use of detailed case studies, allow us to see real people as they adjust, cope, and change in the immigrant context. Yet because case studies are admittedly selective and particularistic, I also provide a broader picture of the larger Dominican population in the United States by drawing on U.S. census and sociological surveys.

My research on Dominicans stretches over a decade. It began in 1980 when I conducted fieldwork in the Dominican Republic on the causes and consequences of outmigration to the United States. This investigation was complemented by several additional years of research among Dominicans in New York (see, Grasmuck and Pessar 1991). In New York my goal was to determine why Dominicans had chosen to settle there in the early '80s and how they were faring in their new home. Now in the '90s, with an ever growing Dominican presence in New York, these remain compelling concerns.

In New York, I have conducted interviews and engaged in participant-observation in scores of homes, workplaces, stores, churches, and schools. In the early '80s I focussed, in particular, on fifty-five immigrant households whose members provided information at regular intervals on a broad range of topics such as migration history, work history, family relations, use of social networks, patterns of socializing, involvement in community associations, and social ties to the Dominican Republic. I sought diversity among these informants, in order to explore how the immigrant experience was affected by such variables as class background, time of arrival, age, marital status, houshold composition, and work history.

Many immigrants are understandably reluctant to speak to strangers, especially one like myself who is perceived to be a member of the dominant society. This reluctance comes from the newcomer's sense of vulnerability in a foreign land, and the fact that some are at clear risk of deportation due to their undocumented status. My ability to gain the trust of people was enhanced, in my view, by my having resided for some time in the Dominican Republic. The experience of having lived there made me especially sensitive to the many losses outmigration represented for my informants, and it exposed me, first hand, to the economic and social problems that propelled many to emigrate.

I used various strategies to identify and contact persons willing to serve as informants. These strategies included reactivating ties with immigrants I had met earlier in the Dominican Republic, using referrals provided by several informants on the island, and relying on introductions extended by other informants and community leaders in New York. I am pleased that, over the years, several relationships that began formally and tentatively have evolved into warm friendships. Along the way I have also endeavored to repay people's help by brokering for them with institutions such as the Immigration and Naturalization Service, social service agencies, schools, and hospitals. If I have managed to bring some humanism and texture to this treatment of Dominicans in the United States, the credit goes, in large part, to the people who generously gave of their time so that I might better understand their struggles, disappointments, and triumphs.

End Notes

1. The title of this book, *A Visa For a Dream: Dominicans in the United States*, is inspired by the popular Dominican merengue, Visa para un Sueño ("Visa For a Dream"), composed by the internationally-acclaimed Dominican musician Juan Luis Guerra.

Dominican Exodus: The Emigration Process

A popular Dominican merengue suggests:

> If petroleum left from here
> There would be light and hope
> Without the need to dream about a visa
> (Juan Luis Guerra, "Si Saliera Petróleo")

Instead of a valued commodity like oil, workers are the island's major export. The overwhelming majority have headed for the United States; and since the late 1960s the Dominican Republic has consistently ranked among the top ten source countries for U.S. immigrants (U.S. Department of Commerce).

The history of outmigration from the Dominican Republic differs significantly from the pattern characteristic of the English-speaking Caribbean, where temporary emigration, within the Caribbean and more recently to England and North America, has been a practice since the 1830s. Large-scale outmigration from the Dominican Republic is a recent phenomena, dating only to the early 1960s. Indeed, over much of the course of Dominican history, the island has been an importer of labor predominantly from the West Indies and Haiti.

Why has the Dominican Republic become a a major exporter of workers? While the bulk of outmigration has been occasioned by economic necessity, the earliest mass migration from the Dominican Republic to the United States was politically-motivated. In 1961 the long dictatorship of Rafael Trujillo (1930-1961) ended with an assassin's bullet. So too did his policy of severely restricting emigration from the island republic. Free elections followed Trujillo's demise and a progressive politician, Juan Bosch, assumed the presidency. Unfortunately, Bosch's social-democratic initiatives, such as modest agrarian reform, quickly ran afoul of the Dominican dominant classes, the military, and the U.S. government. These interests conspired to bring about Bosch's overthrow via a military coup in 1963 (Castro 1985). The coup precipitated several years of unrest and popular uprising culminating in an attempted countercoup led by the Constitutionalists, a coalition led by Bosch's political party and a faction of disaffected young military officers. Heavy fighting ensued, pitting the Constitutionalist military and an increasingly armed civilian population against a more heavily fortified, conservative wing of the Dominican military. When it appeared as if the popular forces might still emerge victorious, the United States decided to intervene militarily. Four thousand marines were dispatched to the Dominican Republic, and although bitter fighting continued for several weeks, the popular revolution was ultimately repelled. There is broad consensus among Dominican and foreign observers that the U.S. military intervention was directed at precluding the establishment of a second Cuba in the United States' backyard. There is also general agreement that the threat of a Communist takeover was vastly exaggerated.

During this politically volatile period Dominican emigration to the United States soared to 9,330 persons per year, up from a yearly average of 990 registered immigrants in the 1950s. Initially the emigrants were largely middle-class people, fearful of the progressive Bosch regime. Soon their concern shifted to the popular unrest gripping the country after the leader's defeat (Guarnizo 1992).

Yet visas were by no means reserved for conservative, middle-class Dominicans. The U.S. ambassador to the Dominican Republic during the early 1960s advocated granting wider access to visas as a safety valve against political agitation and as a way to improve relations between the two countries (Castro 1985; Mitchell 1992). Indeed, he made a personal request for help to the President of the United States and, as a result, obtained new facilities and extra personnel for the consulate in 1962. These measures made it possible for many progressive participants in the Revolution of 1965 to get visas, including members of left-wing and social-democratic parties, labor organizers, and dissident students from the University of Santo Domingo (Georges 1987). Some of these individuals chose to depart for the United States after the defeat of the Constitutionalists. Others were actually deported under the terms of an agreement between the Dominican and U.S. governments (Martin 1966).

Very soon, however, Dominican outmigration ceased being shaped by Dominican and U.S. foreign policy and security concerns. It became more powerfully conditioned by the manner in which the Dominican elite managed state-building and economic planning (Grasmuck and Pessar 1991). Ambitious national programs of state-building and economic modernization, underway since the mid-1960s, raised expectations among all Dominicans for economic advancement. Yet, only a minority benefitted substantially from these programs, leaving far larger numbers sorely tested and disappointed. Rather than forcing their leaders to redesign political and economic policies to meet the economic and social needs of the majority, large numbers of Dominicans have opted instead to seek their fortunes abroad.

The first to rely on a migration-dependent form of state-building and economic development was Joaquín Balaguer, who became president in 1966. Balaguer was successful in gaining the support of both traditional landed elite and a new entrepreneurial and bureaucratic bourgeoisie. He also suppressed virtually all political opposition. In this controlled political climate, Balaguer was able to institute policies and programs that modernized the State (e.g., the professionalization of the armed forces) and the economy. These initiatives resulted in some impressive gains: The gross domestic product (GDP) grew at an annual real rate of 10 percent between 1970 and 1974, one of the highest growth rates in the world during that period.

Socially, the expansion of the urban middle class was one of the most significant changes accompanying the modernization of both the State and the national economy. Since a segment of the Dominican immigrant population originates from this social class, it is useful to consider both its impressive growth and the structural limitations placed on its wellbeing. An indicator of urban, middle-class growth is the rapid change in the nation's occupational structure during the '70s. For example, the number of managers and administrators quadrupled, and professional and technical occupations increased more than one hundred percent over the course of the decade. There was also a tremendous growth in post-secondary education. Enrollment of students pursuing higher education increased from 3,400 in 1960 to 23,500 in 1970, and then skyrocketed to 139,300 in 1982 (Grasmuck and Pessar 1991: 36). These impressive figures indicate a climate of rising expectations for those gaining advanced education. Yet these expectations were often not met.

Despite impressive aggregate statistics of economic prosperity, the majority of Dominicans actually saw their modest incomes decline during the 1970s. For example, a study of income distribution in the capital city of Santo Domingo concluded that the bottom half of the population earned relatively less in 1973 (15.4 percent of the total) than in 1969 (17.6 percent) (ONAPLAN, cited in Grasmuck and Pessar 1991). In practice, this meant that the expanding middle class confronted a very weak internal market for its goods and services. Moreover, the 1970s witnessed an educational mismatch between the supply of well-trained Dominicans and the demand for their skills. In 1979, one out of eight Dominicans residing in the capital who had thirteen years or more of education were unemployed. This figure jumps to one out of five for those with ten to twelve years of education (Ibid: 39). Even among those educated workers who did manage to obtain appropriate-level employment, many were paid salaries which scarcely distinguished them from manual workers. Given these conditions, many middle-class Dominicans sought opportunities abroad.

In the 1980s and 1990s, economic downturns also fueled the drive to emigrate. The Dominican economy was faced with escalating oil prices, a sharp decline in exports, and massive foreign debt that the country could no longer afford to repay. Moreover, national growth rates were negative for the first time in decades. In order to renegotiate its foreign debt, the Dominican government adopted severe structural adjustment measures in 1982 under the tutelage of the International Monetary Fund. These policies dictated a wage freeze that lasted two years and contributed to drastic increases in the cost of basic consumer goods. Not surprisingly, the 1980s witnessed a general pauperization of the population and a shrinking of the middle class (Guarnizo 1992). Indeed, by 1992, per capita income was below levels reached in the early 1970s (when adjusted for inflation); unemployment rose from 15 percent in 1971 to 30 percent in 1991 (Hernández et al. 1995: 14, 16).

Meanwhile the salary differential between the Dominican Republic and the United States continued to widen. In 1980 the minimum monthly salary for full-time work in the United States was four times that of the Dominican Republic; by 1987 the difference had increased to 6 times, and by 1991 to 13 times the republic's minimum wage (Grasmuck and Pessar 1991: 46; Guarnizo 1992: 63). Any Dominican contemplating a move to the United States could only be encouraged by these calculations—and encouraged they were, as the sustained high rates of emigration throughout this period attest (Grasmuck and Pessar 1991). Whereas only 11,655 Dominicans were legally admitted to the United States in 1977, this figure more than doubled throughout much of the 1980s (U.S. Immigration and Naturalization Service 1990). Not only has the volume of migration increased, but so has its socio-economic diversity. The Dominican immigrant stream in the 1960s and 1970s was largely drawn from the middle sectors of Dominican society, but in the 1980s and 1990s it has broadened to include many less-skilled workers and highly skilled professionals (Guarnizo 1992; Grasmuck and Pessar, forthcoming). Nonetheless, the poorest segment of the Dominican population is still underrepresented within this immigrant population.

ORGANIZING EMIGRATION

The social class composition of the Dominican migration stream is not only influenced by political-economic conditions in the Dominican Republic, but also by U.S. immigration and consular policies. The Dominican Republic differs from countries such as Mexico and Jamaica whose rural poor have benefitted from temporary agricultural workers' programs, that both recruit workers and finance their trip abroad. Geography, too, conspires against the Dominican poor. The United States is distant and difficult to penetrate by sea; many who have attempted to reach Florida (or Puerto Rico) by boat have been tragically lost at sea. Consequently, the potential immigrant generally has to obtain some form of visa to enter the United States (Georges 1990). The expenses, social skills, and social contacts involved in acquiring a visa are beyond the reach of many of the very poor.

Visas basically come in two varieties: immigrant (sometimes called residence) and nonimmigrant (tourist and student) visas. A nonimmigrant visa is valid for only a restricted period of time, and under its provisions wage employment is normally forbidden. The immigrant visa is usually valid indefinitely, and confers the right to remunerated employment and to apply ultimately for U.S. citizenship. Most legal immigrants are granted visas under a family unification provision. A lesser number are accepted because they meet the needs of the U.S. labor market for skills in relatively short supply among native-born Americans.

Having been asked by Dominican friends to help them with visa applications, I can personally attest to the often baffling and seemingly endless array of forms involved in the process. In addition to filling out highly bureaucratic forms from the U.S. government, the applicant must also locate and obtain costly local documentation, such as birth, marriage, and health certificates. Many find it necessary to contract the services of a local visa broker or lawyer who is knowledgeable about U.S. immigration law, and knows how to fashion convincing petitions. As one student of Dominican migration recalled, "An application need not be based upon deception, but the fine line between truth and fiction is often not clear.

Embroidery of an individual's work experience may determine his case" (Hendricks 1974: 56). In 1970, *The New York Times* quoted a Dominican lawyer who stated, only half in jest: "After the sugar industry hustling visas has become the biggest business there is in the Dominican Republic" (Ibid: 55). These services did not come cheaply then, and they remain dear today. Many poor Dominicans shy away from even attempting to obtain a visa because they cannot afford fees of many hundreds of dollars and lack the confidence to navigate the visa procurement process alone.

The bulk of legal Dominican immigrants, who have received resident visas, have been beneficiaries of the family unification provision. That is, they are spouses or unmarried children of a permanent resident or spouses, children, parents, or siblings of an adult U.S. citizen (usually one of Dominican birth). For the most part, Dominican immigrants, who initially came from the ranks of the middle and upper working classes, sponsored the immigration of relatives from the same social strata. Thus, the practice of granting visas based on the principle of family unification has tended to reinforce social class selectivity within the Dominican immigrant stream. One man in a small Dominican town told me in 1980, "Only the best families here have emigrated. And it is only a handful, because these families will only marry their children to each other." Of course, in today's world marriage choice has become less the prerogative of status-conscious parents, and more the decision of individual partners who choose "to marry for love." In this manner, Dominican families of more modest means have also been able to take advantage of family unification provisions.

> "Ramón Peralta[1] is a lucky man," I was told. "He may have been born a poor farmer, and he might have even once cursed his fate for being the father of three daughters, who could not help him in the fields. But today he is well-off and retired in New York. His three girls are beautiful, and they easily found [Dominican immigrant] men to marry and take them away from the *campo* (countryside).

In the Peralta family's case, their eldest daughter sponsored her parents' immigration immediately after she became a U.S. citizen. The senior Peraltas and their three daughters have been responsible, in turn, for sponsoring and resettling several other relatively poor family members and close friends.

The second category of immigrant visas, based on labor market needs, is most readily available to individuals with advanced skills or technical knowledge, such as physicians and scientists. While Dominican professionals can apply for such visas, few have sought to emigrate until quite recently when the worsening economic recession has made emigration a far more attractive alternative than in the past. A case in point is Alberto Torres, a middle-aged surgeon, who accepted a position at a small Midwestern hospital and recently moved his entire family abroad. Alberto was acutely aware that he might never gain the prestige he had enjoyed in the Dominican Republic. Nonetheless, he decided to emigrate when the facilities in the hospital where he had worked for many years became so deteriorated that Alberto concluded he could no longer practice "good medicine." Equally important, he found that his hospital salary could not keep up with the rising costs of maintaining an upper-middle-class life style in the Dominican Republic.[2]

Most aspiring Dominican immigrants lack the educational background to apply for a visa based on advanced training and skills. There is, however, another option involving work certification that large numbers of Dominicans have pursued. What typically happens is that close kin or friends in the United States find an employer willing to state that he or she needs immigrant workers—or a particular "alien"—for a job because suitable workers cannot be found in the United States. Juanito Almonte, the husband of one of the Peralta daughters, played just this intermediary role. Employed at a seafood factory on Long Island in the early 1970s, he managed to arrange work authorization documents for three of his wife's male cousins and two of his own close friends from his home town. These new recruits, in turn, helped secure work-related visas for employment in the factory for twelve additional men. In this case emigration cut into the ranks of the unskilled rural sector, since most of the twelve men were agricultural laborers. They were able to emigrate because their Dominican sponsors in the United States assumed responsibility for much of the paperwork and loaned them the money (with interest) to cover their many migration-related expenses.

Those who apply for a nonimmigrant visa need documentation showing they maintain a comfortable standard of living in the Dominican Republic. Consular authorities, charged with deciding whether or not to grant an individual a tourist visa, look for evidence that the applicant has good reason to return to the Dominican Republic. Evidence includes titles to property, such as land or a business, employment in a job paying well over the minimum salary, and a long standing bank account with sufficient funds to defray vacation expenses.

The majority of Dominicans in the United States are residing here legally, but some arrive with fraudulent documentation and others overstay the time period granted for a tourist visa.[3] A smaller segment of the undocumented population are illegal border crossers. Some fly to Mexico City and then cross the border illegally; others stowaway on cargo ships bound for Puerto Rico or south Florida. Sea voyages are notoriously dangerous, leading several Dominican composers and film makers to fashion cautionary tales admonishing their compatriots to avoid this mode of travel. For example, merengue singer, Wilfrido Vargas, warns his listeners to avoid the rickety launches plying the waters between the Dominican Republic and Puerto Rico least they "be eaten by the sharks" ("La Yola").

The costs associated with illegal immigration, such as obtaining fraudulent documentation, are very high—well-over $2,000 in the early 1980s and now as much as $5,000. Consequently, it is the more economically secure who can afford to come illegally, or those who have *personas de confianza* (trusted associates) abroad willing to underwrite the costly and uncertain journey.

Those who possess important know-how ("cultural capital") are also at a decided advantage in successfully managing entry into the United States. Enrique, for example, secured a tourist visa after devising a clever strategy that convinced immigration officials that he would return to the Dominican Republic after visiting relatives in New York. As a young accounting student, he had no permanent job and certainly no savings, yet he had learned from countless friends that immigration officials insisted on a history of well-paid employment and proof of intention to return.

Thus he opened a bank account with money borrowed from three different relatives, and held the account for a few months in order to receive monthly statements of his balance. He also got an uncle, who manages a money-exchange house, to write a letter stating that Enrique had been an employee for several years and would return to his job after his holiday.

On the day of the visit to the U.S. consulate in August 1981, Enrique and his wife, dressed in their finest and armed with the confidence bestowed on university students, easily convinced a consular official to grant them a temporary nonimmigrant visa for recreational travel. One week after arriving in New York, they both secured work as sales clerks in the clothing discount store managed by Enrique's cousin—a store that caters exclusively to Hispanic clients. And, they remained working there long after their tourist visas had expired (Grasmuck and Pessar 1991).

Poorer, less sophisticated Dominicans often have more trouble with officials and may even be too intimidated to try to secure a visa. Irma, an illiterate farmer, became afraid to borrow a cousin's resident visa, or "green card," after her friends told her the plight of a poor *campesino*. The unfortunate peasant, attempting to use a friend's green card, was not only apprehended by airport officials but also lost the money he had spent on his ticket and other travel expenses. Irma concluded that airport officials were far more worldly than she and would trick her into admitting that she was not the person she claimed to be.

These unskilled Dominicans also face a considerable challenge in convincing consular officials that they will readily find and maintain employment in the United States. For their part, U.S. consular officials are pressured to scrutinize all cases carefully to screen out potential welfare recipients (e.g., women intending to travel abroad with young children) or individuals likely to be chronically unemployed. One vice-consul told me of an incident involving a middle-aged day laborer and his interviewer at the American Consulate. The interviewer was apparently highly skeptical about the applicant's chances for managing successfully in the United States. He informed the slightly-built man that he was simply too frail to compete for the backbreaking kinds of jobs that Dominicans of his limited education were finding in New York. Upon hearing this pronouncement, the petitioner arose and proceeded to lift the official's extremely heavy desk off the floor. Both surprised and chastened, the official reversed his decision. There are, however, few such victories for the most vulnerable among the petitioners; indeed, it is the more typical record of failure, which renders the episode of the raised desk eventful and worthy of retelling.

THE "CADENA"

When Dominicans describe emigration to the United States, they speak about the *cadena*, the chain that links one immigrant to the other. Would-be immigrants must either strike out as pioneers and form their own migration chain or seek to link themselves with an established chain, such as the one initiated by the Peralta family.

What links the members of a *cadena*, for the most part, is kinship. Although U.S. immigration policy favors family unification, the definition of the "family" in immigration regulations does not always adequately reflect the network of cooperating kin who constitute the practical and moral family for most Dominicans (see, Garrison and Weiss 1987). This group typically encompasses far more than the immediate nuclear family members who are privileged under U.S. immigration law. It also includes extended kin (such as cousins, aunts, uncles) as well as fictive kin (*compadres*), who are chosen to witness rites of passage, such as baptisms and marriages. In a Caribbean country whose history has been marked by numerous political upheavals and economic crises, the extended family is distinguished as the one group in which strong bonds of trust, cooperation, and affection could be maintained (Hendricks 1974). The history of one *cadena*, that of the Ramírez family, documents the complexity of chain migration. It shows how legal, extra-legal, and illegal migration practices are used, often in highly creative ways, to reunite the socially and culturally meaningful Dominican family.

All *cadenas* begin with a pioneer, and with the Ramírez family it was Willy, the owner of a furniture store in the city of Santiago. In 1975, at the age of 45, he was experiencing problems meeting both the demands of his creditors and mortgage payments on a recently purchased home in an affluent middle-class neighborhood. Having no immediate kin in the United States, Willy contacted a creditor who was also a visa broker (*buscón*). In order to obtain a fraudulent visa from the broker, Willy transferred all the assets from his business, estimated to be approximately 3,000 *pesos* (U.S. $2,200), to the *buscón*.

> "I knew I was taking a big risk," Willy told me. "If I had not made it in New York, perhaps all would have been lost. I wasn't doing this just for my own advancement though, or even that of my wife and children. I was doing it for all my family; many of us had need, but no one was yet in New York to give us a helping hand."

Willy's fraudulent visa got him through U.S. customs. Once in New York, he easily secured a job and housing with the help of a *compadre* who had emigrated a few years earlier. Next, he had to find a way to regularize his legal status so that he might begin petitioning for the admission of his other family members. He decided that his best alternative was to arrange what Dominicans call a *matrimonio de negocio*, a "business marriage." This is a method whereby an individual pays a legal immigrant or citizen a fee to enter into marriage and then uses the family unification provision to acquire a legal resident visa. Such business marriages are meant to be undone; they are sealed by a civil ceremony back in the Dominican Republic, and sexual relations between "business spouses" are proscribed (Georges 1990). It took Willy three years of grueling work at two full-time jobs to save the $2,000 necessary to enter into a "business marriage" with a Dominican co-worker. Willy remained briefly in the Dominican Republic while his "business wife" requested a visa for her "husband," which he soon received. During his short return home, Willy was visited by a first cousin who desperately wanted to migrate abroad. Willy promised to approach his boss in the U.S. for work authorization for the cousin, a promise Willy fulfilled soon after returning to New York.

Willy now had to wait several years, first to divorce his "business wife" and then to remarry his true spouse, Lidia. As is common in the Dominican countryside, Willy and Lidia had married for the first time in a religious ceremony (*matrimonio de la iglesia*). The second time around, they were married in a civil ceremony and Lidia presented only this marriage certificate when she was called sometime later for an interview (*cita*) at the U.S. consulate in Santo Domingo. Lidia's visa was granted in 1983. She immediately joined Willy in the United States, leaving her youngest children with her mother.

While Willy and Lidia planned to save money to sponsor the migration of their youngest children first, unexpected events intervened. In 1985 the husband of Carmen, their 24-year-old daughter, was badly injured at work and she was left with the responsibility of maintaining her immediate family. Unable to find suitable employment, Carmen implored her parents to help her acquire a tourist visa.[4] They sent her funds to contact a local lawyer and money for plane fare. For a fee of several hundred U.S. dollars the lawyer was able to produce sufficient documentation for Carmen (e.g., bank statements and a deed to her home) to convince a Consulate official that she was traveling for recreational purposes and would likely return. With visa in hand, Carmen departed for New York where she moved in with her parents. She easily found employment and, as planned, remained after her tourist visa had expired. Carmen understood that her financial responsibilities encompassed a wide group of kin: her husband and young children back in the Dominican Republic, who had moved in with her mother-in-law, as well as her brothers and sisters, who also sought visas. Her wages were apportioned to meet all these obligations and to contribute to the operating expenses of the Ramírez household in New York.

By 1988, some 13 years after Willy's arrival in New York, he and Lidia were reunited with their three unmarried children. The petitions for these three were comparatively easy and inexpensive since unmarried children of temporary resident aliens are accorded preference under the family unification proviso. Willy also began to fulfill his pledge to help his own siblings. In 1990 he arranged for a poor, widowed sister to come to the United States. He paid $1,000 to a permanent returnee in the Dominican Republic who lent her green card to the widowed sister.

The final step will be for Willy to become a U.S. citizen. As a citizen, Willy will have the right to legally sponsor the emigration of his remaining married children, siblings, and elderly parents. Willy is unhappy about the prospect of renouncing his Dominican citizenship. "I love my country and its flag," he told me "but in the end my family comes first: I am doing it for them, so they can have the same chance I have been given."

The multiple ways that Dominicans, like the Ramírezes, manage to emigrate to the United States are by no means particular to this immigrant population. They represent strategies that are available to, and used by, members of all immigrant-sending societies whose populations view the United States as an economic mecca.

"SI TE VA BIEN, ESCRIBE": "IF THINGS GO WELL THERE, WRITE"

In the Dominican Republic the acquisition of a valid visa takes on a social and cultural worth hardly intended by U.S. officials (Hendricks 1974:67). It is a formal confirmation that the recipient possesses certain social and economic resources valued by a major power like the United States. It is also a badge of success: many will say that the visa recipient has *suerte* ("good luck"), since others with seemingly good documentation have not proved as fortunate. A visa represents both potential and immediate economic power. For example, with visa in hand, most Dominicans have little trouble arranging loans locally prior to emigration, since the lender anticipates an economic windfall for the immigrant shortly after he or she arrives in the United States (Hendricks 1974). That a visa bestows social prestige and privilege was dramatized in a secondary school skit I attended in a rural Dominican town experiencing heavy outmigration. In the skit, the idyllic romance of two young sweethearts was dashed when a young man with an immigrant visa attempted to break up the romance. The more handsome and honest farmer's son simply could not match the marriage proposal and a visa proffered by his rival.

Once they move to the United States, Dominicans experience a great deal of social pressure to prove themselves, perhaps to compensate for the sacrifices their families have made in assisting in the emigration venture. This pressure is captured in the refrain of a popular Dominican merengue about immigration: "If things go well there, write." The clear implication of this refrain is that if things go poorly, the immigrant should not add this failure to the historical record, and perhaps, more to the point should think twice before returning (Grasmuck and Pessar, forthcoming). In this way the successes of immigrants become mythologized and serve to encourage additional outmigration. By contrast, misfortunes are frequently minimized, even buried.

Gustavo, a low-level restaurant worker in New York and the first man to migrate from his rural Dominican town, was both a perpetrator and object of the myth of success. "You would have believed he was Christopher Columbus setting off to discover America," recalled a man from Gustavo's home town. "In fact I remember that most people were frightened for him and many predicted he would never come back." When Gustavo returned in the early 1960s, he was triumphant, well-dressed, and speaking of "his restaurants" in New York. A parade was organized with Gustavo in the lead; and according to community lore, he had "thousands of *pesos* in his pockets." One participant commented, "My God, you'd have thought he was the Pope or something!"

Decades later, most residents of the town continued to perpetuate the fiction of Gustavo's meteoric rise to success,

but the few returnees who had actually lived abroad told another, far more pedestrian tale. They reported that Gustavo
had spent most of his years bussing tables and had never advanced beyond the position of assistant chef. "But by the way
he talked," said a returnee in his town, "we all believed he
owned his own restaurants—not one, but many!" The extent
to which Gustavo intentionally set out to deceive his neighbors, or merely acquiesced to their fantasies about life in New
York, is unclear. More significant, however, is the fact that it
is extremely difficult for returnees to have their accounts of
hardship and struggle accepted and affirmed back home.

> "No one who lives in New York really tells you
> what kind of work they do there, and no one real-
> ly knows what it is like until they've suffered
> there themselves," one returnee explained to me.
> "But you know, even when I tried to tell my fam-
> ily and friends here about how hard it was for me
> there in New York, they kind of looked at me like
> I was trying to keep all the good things for myself.
> So I stopped talking."

The act of mythologizing life and struggles in the United
States is a social and cultural construction that immigrants,
returnees, and those who are left behind create and perpetuate. The fiction of success is so important that some will go to
great lengths to maintain it. For example, when I first met
María López and her two teen-aged daughters, they had recently been abandoned by her husband. María was unemployed and faced eviction from her apartment. Yet needy
relatives in the Dominican Republic continued to call upon
her for money.

> I got a call from my sister last week; you know the
> one who recently had the baby. Well, now she has
> T.B. and she's living on the street. She weighs
> only 80 pounds, is deathly ill, and is trying to take
> care of that infant. She called me collect and asked
> me to send money. She was lucky she was able to
> reach me, because as you know my phone had
> been disconnected for months. I sold my big en-

tertainment unit to get money for the phone bills. It turned out to be a good move, because they've turned off the electricity and we're living with a lantern and candles—like in the *campo*. [She laughs sardonically.] But, if I had told her I had no electricity, we are receiving food stamps, and the girls and I will soon be on the street, she wouldn't have believed me. Everyone there thinks everyone here is rich. So I sold one of the last things of value I have, an emerald ring; and I sent her $100. When I look at all my problems now, I think, where can I go? Where can I escape? I certainly can't go home to add to that misery. I must leave it in God's hands.

In this chapter we mainly focussed on the Dominican Republic: both to account for the reasons why so many Dominicans have emigrated and to explore how they arrange for the journey abroad. We now turn to the United States to consider the contours of Dominican settlement in New York.

END NOTES

1. Here and in most cases I have used pseudonyms to protect the anonymity of my informants.

2. In having located a position in a U.S. hospital, Dr. Torres ranks among the more fortunate of the Dominican-trained physicians. Many of his colleagues have either not attempted to become accredited in the United States (owing sometimes to their undocumented status), or have failed in this attempt. It is estimated that 400 to 500 Dominican physicians are practicing in the New York area, with approximately 70 percent of these doctors concentrated in Washington Heights-Inwood. Others serve the Dominican community by practicing their profession as independent, unlicensed doctors, known as los medicos privados (private doctors). At least another 500 Dominican-trained doctors work in New York in such jobs as paramedics, research assistants, self-employed home

caretakers, and small business owners (Guarnizo 1992: 99).

3. It is estimated that in 1992, approximately 40,000 undocumented Dominicans resided in the United States (Warren 1994: 29).

4. As a married woman, Carmen was not eligible to be petitioned as a dependent child by her parents. And even if she had been successful in hiding the fact of her marriage, she was not in the financial position to wait a year or more for a temporary resident visa.

2

Settling in New York

The ties of responsibility and obligation linking members of an immigrant *cadena* rarely terminate once a visa is granted. In fact, social relations usually intensify as the sponsor assumes an important role in anchoring the newcomer to his or her new home. The sponsor is often the one who meets the new arrival at the airport and arranges for temporary lodging. Such was the case for Gertrudes Pérez, a 33 year old, who emigrated to the United States in 1981. She recalled how nervous she was when she got out of customs, afraid to be alone with no English and no real sense of where she was. "But there just outside the gates was my brother, just like my guardian angel." He and his family applauded as she passed through the gates, and one of Gertrudes' nieces ran up with a bouquet of flowers. Gertrudes then lived with her brother and his family for about a year in their Washington Heights apartment, sleeping in a small bed with one of her nieces, and contributing to the family's rent and other household expenses.

As Gertrudes' case illustrates, Dominican immigrant households tend to be very flexible and accommodating of new arrivals; Indeed, it would be virtually inconceivable for established immigrants to request a relative or close friend to reside in a commercial establishment or alone during the initial period of settlement. "There is always room for one more," Gertrudes' brother told me, "even if it means having the children double up or sleep on the sofa. We are a people who put family first." His statement is corroborated by a 1980 survey of Dominicans in New York, which found that recent immigrants tended to live in extended households with kin who were often not members of their immediate nuclear families. Only later in the immigrant process did Dominican New Yorkers tend to recreate nuclear households (Gilbertson and Gurak 1992).[1]

Sponsors, and other close kin or friends, also attempt to find employment for the newcomer. Few are immediately whisked off to work as immediately as the protagonist in a merengue who complains that he is met at the airport by a cousin who "instead of inviting [him] for a drink," takes him to work at a factory (Luis Kallaff, "Un Cibaeno en Nuevo York"). Yet, in the past, jobs often awaited the immigrant or were found in a matter of days. Gertrudes' sister-in-law found her a job at the lamp factory where she worked. "I was really amazed; after months of finding no work back home, I was making lamps in a factory and making good money— $3.75 an hour after being in New York for less than a week."

Of course the role of social networks in directing new-comers to employment opportunities is ultimately only as effective as the overall demand for immigrant workers. Consequently, in 1991, some ten years after Gertrudes' arrival in New York, she experienced some difficulty in finding a job for her newly-arrived daughter. Whereas Gertrudes had found a job immediately, her daughter Mercedes remained unemployed for more than three months before locating work as a waitress in a restaurant owned by a distant cousin. As Chapter 3 will demonstrate, this contrast reflects recent changes in the New York economy that have reduced employment opportunities for many Dominicans. There is the expectation that when assistance to the newcomer comes from close kin, it should be extended altruistically without a concern for possible profit. It is also anticipated that all monetary expenditures made on behalf of the immigrant, as well as services rendered (e.g., locating housing and a job), will be ultimately repaid in cash or in kind. Nonetheless, some established Dominicans have been known to profit from their recently arrived kin. Ana Rosario, who knew that I was friendly with eight of the disgruntled in-laws whom she had recently assisted, had this to say about her assistance:

> My husband's family expects our help as a *regalo* (gift). They did not like it when I charged them $350 each for their papers, and when I charge them two percent interest per month on the money we lent them to make the trip and get settled. But to succeed your money has to be circulating and making more money. I work real hard for my money and work hard to help others get ahead too; but I won't do it for charity. They don't need charity; they work just like me.

In Ana's case, sponsorship, both before and after emigration, brought substantial rewards. In charging her kin $350 per person for acquiring needed documentation, Ana reaped $2,800. She also housed all eight family members, some for several months, others for over one year. At a monthly charge of $85 per person, the rent (for the eight) more than covered her mortgage and utility bills. She stated that she was earning some additional "pocket money" on the interest she was charging her kin for their loans. While Ana's behavior is hardly unique, it is also not typical. In fact, one of Ana's relatives told me privately that in charging her kin so much for her services, Ana was being selfish and mean-spirited to folks who were, in his words, "just off the banana boat."

NEW YORK: THE CAPITAL OF DOMINICANS ABROAD

Even back in the late 1960s when anthropogist Glenn Henricks conducted his pioneering study of Dominican immigration to New York, he observed that immigrants seldom arrived as social isolates, forced to cope with the new environment alone. "The very nature of the process of recruitment into the United States almost obliges the individual to have some preexisting social linkages to New York" (Hendricks 1974: 73). To this day New York remains the magnet for most Dominicans as newcomers continue to be recruited into the social networks established by earlier cohorts. According to the 1990 U.S. Census, 70 percent of all persons of Dominican ancestry resided in New York. The Empire State was followed by neighboring New Jersey with 11 percent; Florida with 7 percent, and Massachusetts with 5 percent (Hernández et al.: 6). In other words, 93 percent of the Dominicans living in the United States resided in only four states. In Alejandro Portes and Rubén Rumbaut's words, "Migration is a network-driven process, and the operation of kin and friendship ties is nowhere more effective than in guiding new arrivals toward preestablished ethnic communities" (Portes and Rumbaut 1990: 32).

New York City hosts the largest concentration of Dominicans outside of their home island of Hispaniola. In 1990, a total of 332,713 were reported to be living in New York City, comprising 65 percent of the total Dominican population in the U.S. (Hernández et al.: 7). This is, however, a disputed figure. Dominican leaders insist that many undocumented Dominicans have avoided the Census takers and argue that the true number of Dominicans in New York City is twice or three times as large as the "official" count. What is undisputed is that the number of Dominicans in New York City has grown tremendously. A mere 9,223 were enumerated in the city's 1960 Census, placing Dominicans in 26th place among immigrant populations there. In stark contrast, they currently enjoy first place (Guarnizo 1992). Over the decade of the '80s New York City's Dominican population increased by 165 percent, a gain unmatched by any other major ethnic group (Hernández et al.: 8). The bulk of this growth has been due to immigration; in fact, of the 206,719 foreign-born Dominicans recorded in the 1990 New York City Census, more than one-half arrived over the decade of the 1980s (Grasmuck and Pessar, forthcoming)

SETTLEMENT PATTERNS

Distinct settlement patterns within the New York metropolitan area have evolved over time. Like European immigrants from an earlier era, Dominicans first congregated in Manhattan's Lower East Side where they were attracted to cheap housing and jobs in manufacturing and services. In the late 1960s Dominicans could find three-room apartments for as little as $35 a month, and they could walk to jobs in local apparel factories (Hendricks 1974). The Lower East Side was also one of the sites of Puerto Rican settlement and many Dominican "pioneers" acknowledge the initial assistance Puerto Ricans extended to them.

> "Now there is a Spanish-speaker on every corner," said one man who arrived in 1962, "but back then if you got lost, if you needed help, you might have to search for hours and even then it was likely that you would not find anyone who could understand you....In those early years, we Dominicans were helped a lot by Puerto Ricans who already knew the ropes. I and most of my friends started out by living as boarders with Puerto Rican families. Puerto Ricans also helped us when we needed our own apartment or a job. In fact I got one of my first jobs from a Puerto Rican neighbor.

Unfortunately, the Lower East Side was also notorious for being overcrowded and disreputable. One woman described her early years in the neighborhood:

> When we first arrived in New York I was eight years old. We lived just blocks away from the Bowery and every day on my way to school I had to pass filthy drunks who sometimes cursed me. I was always scared, and kept asking my mother why we came and when we were going back home.

Over the course of the 1960s, the more financially secure Dominicans rejected the squalor and decay of the Lower East Side and began to seek out middle-class neighborhoods in Queens (e.g., Corona) and Long Island (e.g., Rockville Center). These pioneers in turn became magnets for others from their home towns and villages. Indeed, the mass resettlement of large numbers of Dominicans from specific locales has given rise to the "Dominicanization" of U.S. place names. Corona, Queens, for example, is fondly referred to as *Sabana Church* due to the large number of residents originally from the Dominican community of Sabana Iglesias (Hendricks 1974).

Another locale whose name has been appropriated and Dominicanized is the Upper Manhattan neighborhood of Washington Heights, or "Quisqueya Heights" (Quisqueya being the indigenous name of the Dominican Republic). Stretching north on the west side of New York City from roughly 145th Street to 190th, the neighborhood is reputed to be the home of approximately one-third of all Dominicans in New York City; and it has emerged as the heart of the Dominican community in New York. In the past Washington Heights received successive waves of immigrants and migrants from Ireland, Eastern Europe, Puerto Rico, and Cuba; it still remains the home of many ethnic groups. Nonetheless, today it is Dominicans who have placed their distinctive stamp on the cultural forms and institutions they have encountered, and who have, in turn, been challenged and changed by the social and cultural lifeways they have confronted in Washington Heights.

WASHINGTON HEIGHTS

The Dominican presence is clearly felt in the economic life of Washington Heights, where Dominican-owned businesses are burgeoning and the blend of Dominican and American elements is striking. Were you to enter a local Dominican *bodega* (small neighborhood market), its name would likely combine both Spanish and English words, such as in *"Puerto Plata Market"* or *"Tres Amigos Deli."* Bodegas are stocked with a variety of main line American brands, items produced for the U.S. Hispanic market (e.g., Goya can goods), Dominican staples such as *plátanos* (plantains), and Dominican brand names (e.g., Quisqueya cola, Presidente beer). While American-manufactured pharmaceuticals are available, so are certain roots (e.g., *maguel*) and tropical plants needed to make medicinal teas. Corner newsstands sell numerous Dominican newspapers, flown daily from the island, alongside locally printed Spanish and English-language publications. If you were to dine at one of the many Dominican restaurants, you might find hamburgers on the menu; but Dominican specialties, such as *sancocho*, *mangú*, and *carne guisada* would surely predominate.

The presence of these numerous and diverse Dominican-owned enterprises demonstrates the existence of a Dominican ethnic economy centered in Washington Heights. One recent study of Washington Heights estimated that there are between 1,500 and 2,000 visible Dominican-owned enterprises (Guarnizo 1992: 112). In addition to the neighborhood *bodegas* and restaurants specializing in *comida criolla* (Dominican cuisine), other local businesses include travel agencies, money transfer agencies (*envíos*), shops offering long distance telephone services, beauty salons, clothing stores, laundromats, pharmacies, and non-medallion "gypsy" cab operations.

Dominicans are also leaving their mark on neighborhood schools. Here Dominicans have had to struggle collectively to establish a respected place and powerful voice. Yolanda López still speaks passionately about the campaign in the early 1980s to gain greater community control over the schools in Washington Heights (Community School District 6), and to make the neighborhood schools more responsive to the needs and aspirations of their Dominican residents. "Even in the early '80s, our kids made up the bulk of students in the schools. But at that time our schools were the most over-crowded in the city, and many of our children left school without knowing how to read. We realized no one would help our kids if we Dominican parents did not struggle to take control."

The movement for empowerment and control in District 6 began in 1980 when the Community Association of Progressive Dominicans confronted the school board and superintendent to demand bilingual education and programs for recently-arrived immigrant families. Over the years Dominicans have gained a greater representation on the school board and have consequently been able to tailor programs to meet the needs of newcomers more effectively. Their success has been the product of an aggressive program of voter registration, the creation of a parents' network throughout the District (based in the parent associations in each school), and the formation of a coalition of parents, community organizations, churches, and educators (Linares 1989). Other gains have included the construction of additional public schools in the extremely over-crowded district, and in 1994 the appointment of a Dominican principal to head the community high school (three-quarters of whose student body is Dominican). It is a fitting commentary on the emerging presence of Dominicans in New York and the United States that the Dominican principal presides over George Washington High School!

At the same time, many Dominican parents remain justly concerned with what they view as a decline in educational performance in the district, and with a failure to maintain discipline in the neighborhood public schools. When Euclid Mejía took over as principal of George Washington High school, it was one of only six schools in the city whose low test scores and high drop-out rates provoked threats of a takeover by the Chancellor of the New York City Schools (New York Newsday 1994: 15). As a result of these problems, many Dominicans in Washington Heights have elected to send their children to parochial schools, and children with behavioral or learning problems are frequently sent back to the Dominican Republic for their education.

Concerns go beyond children's poor school performance, however, to a preoccupation with the general deterioration in public services and an increase in neighborhood violence and crime (González 1993). The existence of a thriving drug trade in Washington Heights is clearly on many people's minds. Among the drug industry's most unfortunate victims are those Dominican youth who participate in the distribution and sale of cocaine. In a recent study of a teeenage drug ring located in Washington Heights, the author had this to say:

> Money and drugs are the obvious immediate rewards for kids in the cocaine trade. But there is another strong motivating force,...the desire to show family and friends that they can succeed at something. Moving up a career ladder and making money is especially important where there

> are few visible opportunities....Washington
> Heights, which the police call a "hot spot," is a
> battleground in the war on drugs. And as in all
> wars, it is the young who are the first casualties
> (Williams 1989: 10, 26).

While recognizing that only a small segment of the community is involved in the sale or use of drugs, Dominican
leaders have called for a concerted community effort to confront this problem.

> In the 1970s,...it was an issue mainly of deal-
> ing....They would tell you that I don't use drugs,
> all I do is sell it to the white people who come
> from Jersey. Well, that has changed completely.
> Now what we have are a lot of young crack ad-
> dicts, young crack addicts among Dominicans
> (Gilbertson 1995: 8).

Dominicans will have to increase their political power in
New York City to confront this and other problems facing
their community. There are many hopeful signs of an increased political presence and influence. The struggle to gain
greater control over the neighborhood schools marked an important step in political mobilization. In the words of Guillermo Linares, a Dominican activist who served as head of the
school board, "The education struggle and Community
School Board Elections are important vehicles for empowering the community, especially Dominicans and Latinos, who
cannot vote in regular elections, but who can vote in school
board elections" (Linares 1989:84). His words proved to be
prophetic: in 1991 Linares was the first Dominican-born person elected to the New York City Council, where he represented the newly-redistricted community of Washington
Heights. Dominicans continue to hold influential positions in
city government and local community development. Such
strides in political participation and representation were
greatly facilitated by early efforts at community-building on
the part of Dominican ethnic organizations, many of which
were established in Washington Heights. Indeed, one re-
searcher counted some 125 Dominican voluntary associations

in the Washington Heights-Inwood area in the mid 1980s (Georges 1988). Candidates for community and city government have emerged from the ranks of Dominican ethnic associations, and these organizations have been used to mobilize funds and votes (Goris-Rosario 1994).

The religious life of Washington Heights also has a decidedly Dominican cast. Many homes feature small altars devoted to Catholic saints, such as the Virgin of Altagracia, patron saint of the Dominican Republic. Like other Hispanic Catholics, many Dominicans believe that the saints will protect them from harm and help in their social advancement (Duany 1994). Some years back I was invited by a Dominican friend to a banquet organized to repay the Virgin of Altagracia for helping her children to obtain visas. Magaly explained that she prayed to the Virgin because the saint is very powerful, and Magaly needed a lot of help with immigration officials because many petitions for children were being denied. "The Virgin heard my prayers," she stated, "and I am fulfilling my obligation by honoring her with a fiesta."

Several local Catholic churches which once labored to integrate earlier waves of Puerto Ricans into their predominately Irish and Italian congregations have now emerged as Dominican parishes. As such, these churches are especially responsive to the beliefs and practices of their Dominican practitioners. They hold mass in Spanish and invite religious officials from the the island to participate in church activities. One Washington Heights church has even been named Our Lady of Altagracia. Perhaps because the Catholic Church has helped ease Dominicans' adjustment to U.S. society, participation rates at Sunday Mass among Dominican immigrants are far higher than those for Dominicans back home. Yet while the neighborhood churches foster a sense of continuity and belonging to a Dominican ethnic community, the Catholic Church also offers a bridge to the wider society, as, for example, when Dominicans journey downtown to attend the annual celebration of the Virgin of Altagracia (Our Lady of the Highest Grace) at New York's Saint Patrick's Cathedral (Goris-Rosario 1994).

Washington Heights also supports new cultural forms that draw upon the immigrant and working-class experiences of the Dominican diaspora. There is a flourishing cultural movement comprised of many groups that promote Dominican poetry, theater, music, fine arts, and dance. In *Historias de Washington Heights Y Otros Rincones Del Mundo/ Stories From Washington Heights and Other Corners of the World*, co-editor Daisy Coco de Filippis observes that the Dominican authors included in this pioneering collection struggle with experiences of exile and transience. They experience exile as a search for "la casa materna" (the maternal home) "in these foreign lands and ways." By writing they begin, "to change words into stones; to find an anchor for their homesickness and their longing for permanence and a place for being" (Coco De Filippis and Gutiérrez 1994: 16).

In their private lives, Dominicans, like other recent immigrants, remain committed to a variety of cultural practices brought from home. For example, a recent study of Dominican households in Washington Heights found that 95 percent cooked mostly Dominican food, 88 percent spoke mostly Spanish at home, and well over half listened mostly to Dominican music and watched mostly Spanish television (Duany 1994: 37). Similarly, when Dominicans have some free time, they are most apt to socialize with family and Dominican friends. While some apartment dwellers complain about being isolated in their own units ("trancado," "locked in), others have managed to forge a small community in their buildings, uniting with neighbors in frequent exchanges of favors, mutual aid, and emotional support (Ibid: 22).

ETHNIC SUCCESSION IN WASHINGTON HEIGHTS

Ethnic succession within U.S. neighborhoods and communities is rarely characterized by harmony and consensus. The many gains Dominicans have made in Washington Heights have not come without challenge to other established ethnic and racial groups in the community. The Dominican struggle to control the neighborhood schools, for example, came largely at the expense of the community's Jewish population, who despite their relatively small numbers, dominated the district's school board until they were ousted by Dominicans (Lowenstein 1989). Although members of the Jewish community first tried to protect their vested interests by blocking the educational, economic, and political advances of newcomers to Washington Heights, a position of resigned accommodation now prevails. As one Jewish leader stated:

> In order to save our...own congregation, we have to live with our neighbors, even if they are different from us, even if we don't like them. But we cannot help it. We have to live with the blacks, with the Spanish (Ibid: 321).

Tensions also exist between Dominicans and Puerto Ricans. Some Puerto Ricans criticize Dominicans for allegedly accepting low wages, thereby undercutting Puerto Ricans in the job market. Angry voices are also raised against Dominicans and their Puerto Rican "accomplices" for displacing Puerto Ricans as owners of neighborhood *bodegas*. In the words of Ramón Velez, a Puerto Rican community leader, 6,500 "Puerto Rican Judases, sold their *bodegas* to Dominicans in New York City (Guarnizo 1992: 107). Dominicans, in turn, often accuse Puerto Rican law enforcement agents and code inspectors of discrimination and abuse of power in their treatment of Dominicans (Guarnizo 1992). There is also the belief among some Dominicans that they are being held back in politics and community organizations by a Hispanic leadership that pursues a narrrowly Puerto Rican agenda (Grasmuck and Pessar, forthcoming). "We all sit at the table when it comes time to draw lines [between Latinos and the others]," one Dominican politician stated. "When the time comes to determine who represents all of us, we no longer find ourselves at the table" (González 1992:B4). There is also concern over the apportioning of funds for the two groups. Another Dominican leader noted:

> The Puerto Rican community has said we only get 3% of the state budget, the other 97% goes to white groups, African-American groups....In the same way that the Puerto Rican community [says they] deserve a better share because [they] are 9

or 10% of the state and only get 3% of the budget[,] we say, well, we are 25% of the Latinos and we get only 2% of the Latino budget (Gilbertson 1995: 11).

Although Dominican youth borrow elements of Afro-American culture and add them to their music, language, and dress, social encounters between Dominicans and African-Americans in Washington Heights can be confrontational. Contacts are frequently made in Dominican-owned, neighborhood businesses, where "African-Americans regard Dominican business owners more as adversarial, foreign merchants taking advantage of blacks' disadvantaged economic condition than as dark-skinned immigrants struggling for survival" (Guarnizo 1992: 109).

CONCLUSION

This chapter has focussed on social networks, both those linking individual immigrants and those which become far more densely enmeshed and linked to a particular locale, thereby creating an ethnic community like Washington Heights. The existence of vital ethnic communities, like Washington Heights, are crucial to the continued recruitment and maintenance of newer immigrants even after the favorable economic conditions promoting mass emigration have diminished or ceased.

END NOTES

1. The generosity extended by Dominicans to newly-arrived family and friends can cause problems, as well. Several of my informants complained of inadequate space for their children to play and study and escalating conflict among family members due to overcrowding. Indeed, a few of my informants temporarily shared cramped quarters with two or three families in apartments designed for only one.

3

Buscando Mejor Vida: In Search of a Better Life

If most Dominicans have come to the United States in search of a better life, why have they headed to New York City? New York's labor market, after all, has witnessed a general decline in employment over the very same decades that Dominican emigration has been most massive. Yet, at the same time, the city has witnessed a profound economic restructuring, one that offers some new possibilities. While there has been a reduction in the number of stable, unionized jobs, there has also been a proliferation of menial, insecure, and low-paying jobs in manufacturing, trade, and services. These low-end jobs have attracted new immigrants, while many blue-collar, native-born workers have left New York in pursuit of better employment prospects elsewhere (Waldinger 1987).

New York City's economic restructuring occurred in the face of heavy competition from other domestic and international markets. The manufacturing industry, long a pillar of the local economy, included many businesses that either would not or could not afford to retain native-born workers by increasing wages and improving working conditions. Manufacturers also failed to invest in modern equipment and technology, which might have reduced their reliance on labor. Many firms ultimately shut down or relocated elsewhere; others, however, found a solution in the supply of new immigrants willing to accept prevailing wage levels and working conditions, and often possessing the skills needed in traditional manufacturing industries. An increasing reliance on immigrants put a brake on escalating wages and operational costs. For example, the apparel industry, a major beneficiary of immigrant labor, actually experienced a 10 percent decline in average hourly wages between 1965 and 1980 (Waldinger 1983:111). One study concludes that the large number of new immigrants has actually increased the demand in manufacturing for these workers (Marshall 1983). Employers have come to rely on labor-intensive techniques and older forms of production, such as subcontracting and industrial homework, which depend on a cheap and compliant workforce.

DOMINICANS IN THE NEW YORK CITY ECONOMY

Dominicans have found a niche in New York City's restructured manufacturing industries. In 1979, almost one half (49%) of all Dominican workers, but only 18 percent of New York City's total labor force were engaged in manufacturing. A decade later the percentage of Dominicans working in manufacturing declined to 26 percent, yet it was still much higher than the percentage of all New York City workers in this sector (12 percent) (Hernández et al. 1995: 42-45).[1] The Dominican niche in manufacturing is a mixed blessing. For some, like Marcela Espinal, employment in the manufacturing sector has proved to be relatively secure and even permitted modest economic advancement. Marcela has progressed over the years from a sewing machine operator to a highly skilled, well-paid sample maker. For most Dominicans, however, employment in the garment industry offers little if any chance for improving wages or responsibility (See Pessar 1984; 1994). To the contrary, many Dominican women and men have faced an increasing risk of underemployment and unemployment as jobs have been lost in apparel and other manufacturing industries. Over 520,000 manufacturing jobs in New York City disappeared between 1967 and 1987 alone (Hernández et al. 1995: 41).

Dominicans, like other New Yorkers, clearly distinguish between "good" and "bad" manufacturing jobs. Marcela's job, with its comparatively high wages, generous benefits package, and modest opportunities for advancement, is considered a "good" job. Unfortunately, a central tenet of industrial restructuring is the replacement of "good" manufacturing jobs by "bad" ones, such as those found in the growing subcontracting sector. Thus, while Dominicans may manage to find jobs in New York's manufacturing industry, there has been a marked deterioration in the quality of life such jobs afford, as Tinita Hernández's job history demonstrates.

Tinita found employment in a unionized garment factory soon after she arrived in New York City in 1973. Although she divorced her husband a few years later, Tinita's earnings permitted her to live very modestly with her two young daughters in a rented apartment in Washington Heights. Things changed for the worse in 1980 when, complaining of lagging sales due to foreign competition, her employer closed the business. Tinita struggled for a few months on unemployment benefits while she awaited word of a new job through her contacts at the International Ladies Garment Workers Union. When a unionized job was not forthcoming, Tinita reluctantly accepted a friend's offer to find her work as a seamstress in a non-unionized subcontracting shop.

Tinita's reluctance grew out of the fact that wages and working conditions in subcontracting shops are usually far inferior to those in manufacturing firms, which transfer much of the risk in today's apparel market down the line to the subcontractors. The subcontractors, in turn, pass on their risks and losses to workers who often earn below minimum wages and are deprived of benefits such as social security and worker's compensation. For Tinita, the change from employment in a manufacturing firm to a subcontracting shop meant precarious earnings and the lack of the safety net that benefits, such as health insurance, had previously afforded her family. When her new job was able to provide full-time work, Tinita's weekly wages scarcely covered her rent, utilities, and food bills. Yet, during the garment industry's off-season (September-January), the shop frequently shut down completely due to lack of business, leaving Tinita compelled to borrow money from relatives to make ends meet. This was the case, even though she had taken in a female boarder who contributed $100 a month toward the $250 rental fee. Tinita's daughters now had to double up with their mother in her tiny bedroom. Tinita sorely missed her health insurance benefits, since she could rarely afford to refill subscriptions for costly ulcer medication. The last time I visited Tinita in her home in 1985, she showed me a greatly overdue hospital bill received after a particularly painful attack of ulcers had forced her to the emergency room. She asked my help in convincing a hospital social worker to wave the fee, a concession that was fortunately granted.

The restructuring of New York City's manufacturing industry has held greater promise for Dominican immigrant entrepreneurs. Operations such as apparel subcontracting shops require relatively little start-up capital and thus are within the reach of immigrant investors. In a recent study of Dominican entrepreneurs in New York, sociologist Luis Guarnizo found that 12 percent of the 92 firms he sampled were dedicated to manufacturing (1992: 121). Many of the owners (especially garment and leather manufacturers) started out as piece-rate workers, rose to supervisory positions, and finally set off on their own as subcontractors (Ibid: 113). While the net worth of several of the businesses included in Guarnizo's study was modest (less than $30,000), he did find a few firms with assets of one million dollars or more (Ibid: 261). Let us examine one such micro-enterprise.

Argentina Flores' movement into the ranks of small proprietor started inauspiciously in 1979, when her boss closed down the sewing department of the sportswear factory where she had worked for many years. The boss then alerted Argentina of his plan to subcontract the work that had previously been performed in her department. "He said he valued my loyalty and my skills; he arranged to loan me some of his machines at a very low interest rate so that I could begin a small sewing operation in my basement." Argentina immediately contacted ten of her former co-workers who remained unemployed. Three were willing to work for her at wages that were significantly below those they had earned in the sportswear factory. She filled out her roster of five employees by hiring a neighbor and one of her cousins. Argentina obtained most of her work from her ex-boss, although an occasional order came from one of his business associates. When I interviewed Argentina in 1981, she estimated, perhaps optimistically, that she would turn a profit of approximately $12,000 at year's end. In purely monetary terms, this represented a gain over her earnings as an apparel worker, which totaled about $9,000 in 1979. Moreover, Argentina was already talking enthusiastically about collaborating with a male cousin to purchase a twenty-worker garment operation, which was then being sold by a Dominican acquaintance who was returning home.

While Argentina's profits were modest, her aspirations were grand. Only a select few, however, have turned such lofty aspirations into reality. They include Mr. Martínez, the Dominican owner of a 130-worker garment plant, who routinely obtains contracts from major U.S. corporations, such as J C Penny (Guarnizo 1992). Unfortunately, when I last spoke to Argentina in 1990, I learned that her small sewing operation had failed due to a lack of business and a sufficiently stable workforce. She had been working since 1983 as a sewing machine operator in the shop of one of her previous clients.

Dominican immigrants have also found jobs in New York City's retail and wholesale trades. In 1979 one out of five Dominican workers was employed in this sector; by 1989 the ratio had jumped to over one in four (28 percent). The extreme concentration of Dominicans in retail and wholesale trades (more than any other racial and ethnic group in the city) has meant that Dominicans have been especially affected by declines in this sector, which lost over 106,000 jobs in New York City between 1967 and 1987 (Hernández et al.: 41).

Many Dominicans have established their own retail businesses, perhaps the most visible example being the *bodeguero*. Dominican *bodega* owners and the proprietors of somewhat larger *supermercados* (supermarkets) were featured in an article in *The New York Times*, whose headline proclaimed, "Dominicans Thrive Where Big Chains Won't Go" (Myerson 1992: C1). A few years later a more sober article was captioned, "New York's Bodegas Become Islands Under Siege"

(Bragg 1994: B39). It emphasized the great physical risks most *bodegueros* and their employees face, and featured Domingo León, a 40-year old Dominican, who arrived in New York in the early '70s and opened a *bodega* some twelve years later with his own savings. "This is a dream to me," Mr. León told the reporter. He went on to explain that a person who has never been poor cannot appreciate what it means to him to hold the keys to his livelihood and not have to bow his head to anyone. But, he added somberly that he fears that one day he will die defending his dream. Mr. León, like scores of other Dominican bodegueros, had a harrowing, first-hand experience with, what in "Spanglish" is called "holopes" (holdups). In 1992 alone, 47 bodega owners and employees were killed by "holoperos" (robbers) in New York City (Ibid).

In addition to dealing with the threat of violence, *bodegueros* must also maintain a grueling work schedule. Many businesses are open seven days a week, from 7 in the morning until midnight or later. The owner must arrive at the Bronx Terminal Market (*La Marketa*) at around 4 a.m. at least three times a week to purchase fresh produce; he or she typically closes the store much later that night (Guarnizo 1992). In order to cope with these extreme demands, many Dominican New Yorkers run their businesses with the help of trusted, extended family members. The struggle to keep businesses afloat may also force some to engage in illicit practices such as selling illegal lottery tickets (the *bolita*) and bootlegged Dominican rum. Those involved in such illegal activities run the risk of discovery by government officials and fines they can ill afford, but this risk is part of business-as-usual for those entrepreneurs forced to find ways to survive at the margins.[2]

Dominican New Yorkers are also increasingly found in jobs in the city's service sector, an industry that has recently emerged as the largest employer of workers in New York City. Immigrants from all groups have found opportunities for low-paid employment in the advanced, highly specialized service sector and in other service activities meeting the needs of the city's high income professionals (Sassen 1991). In 1989 the service industry ranked as the largest employer of Dominican laborers, with over 28 percent of the entire Dominican workforce (Hernández et al.: 43). Some Dominicans with college and graduate educations have been able to take advantage of the increase in lucrative, white-collar jobs in this sector. Most, however, compete for more modest employment. With only eighth-grade educations, Gloria and Iván Espinal, count themselves fortunate for having been employed since 1973 as orderlies in a large nursing home. With their accumulated savings, they have purchased homes in New York and in the Dominican Republic, and they have sent their three children to college. By contrast, Gloria's newly-arrived sister earns less than the minimum wage in her job as a live-in caretaker for an elderly Puerto Rican woman. "The ones who came earlier are the ones who have really succeeded," Marta stated, gesturing in her sister's direction. "For newcomers like me, what do we do? Work to eat and maybe to send a few *pesitos* (dollars) home."

The service industry is also popular among Dominican entrepreneurs. Almost half of the Dominican-owned firms surveyed by Guarnizo were in the service sector, typically small operations with a net worth under $10,000 (1992: 121, 220). Such ventures include gypsy cab operations; beauty salons; and small businesses offering discount phone services to the Dominican Republic.

DECLINING OPPORTUNITIES

In the last ten years or so, jobs have become far less secure and attractive than in the past. There has been a general decline in manufacturing jobs in New York as a result of industrial restructuring. Local businesses have struggled with the larger economic recession, and as a consequence, many Dominican workers have had to face longer and more frequent episodes of work slow downs and temporary lay-offs, as well as job loss due to business closings. As we have seen, Dominicans are concentrated in two sectors, manufacturing and wholesale/retail trades, which have been especially fraught with massive job loss. The recent arrival of new populations of immigrants, who are willing to accept even lower wages and more inferior working conditions than many Dominicans deem acceptable, has also negatively affected the employment picture. Ironically, back in the '60s and '70s, Puerto

Ricans could be heard complaining of unfair competition and job loss at the hands of new Dominican immigrants who were willing to work for extremely low wages in a shrinking New York labor market. Today it is Dominicans who express similar concerns about newly arrived Mexicans and Central Americans, who are allegedly displacing Dominicans from their niche in certain low wage industries (Guarnizo 1992). Although the growth of Dominican businesses has created employment opportunities, jobs in Dominican-owned business tend to pay less and provide less adequate health and retirement benefits than those in native-owned firms (Grasmuck and Pessar 1991; Gilbertson and Gurak 1993).[3]

Given this somber picture, it may seem surprising that most Dominicans have arrived in New York during the last fifteen years. While economic opportunities for Dominican New Yorkers may be less attractive than they were in the earlier decades of emigration, remember that they still compare favorably to the massive unemployment, underemployment, and ever declining value of real wages in the Dominican Republic. Indeed, by 1991 the purchasing power of the minimum wage in the Dominican Republic represented one-half of the value it had enjoyed in the early 1970s (Hernández et al.: 16); not surprisingly, consumption per capita fell by 22 percent between 1982 and 1992 (Ibid: 14). Also, the presence of employed kin in New York allows individuals to contemplate and weather a stint of unemployment in New York. Laura Moya, for example, arrived in New York in 1991 to find that the job she thought was awaiting her in the factory where her mother worked, had been given to a Mexican immigrant. Laura spent four months searching for another factory job, while her mother covered all of her expenses. Of course, despite economic downturns in New York, the visual images of life in the United States that Dominicans on the island receive via cable and advertising remain strong inducements to migrate. Manuel Pérez left a good job and his university studies despite his mother's admonitions. As she told me:

> "He is young and all he sees on T.V. back home are American programs that show elegant clothes, luxurious homes, and fancy cars. So he

thinks, this is New York. I told him to stay back home, because it isn't so; there was nothing but hard work and low pay if you're lucky enough to find work. But he didn't listen; he had to see for himself and suffer."

A Profile of Dominicans in New York

Mrs. Pérez's claim that her son would "suffer" in New York is not merely a rhetorical flourish voiced by an understandably distraught mother. The economic condition of Dominican New Yorkers is worse than other New Yorkers, including other Hispanics, according to the 1990 Census. The Dominican population had the highest poverty rate, 37 percent compared to 17 percent for the entire city, and 31 percent for all Hispanics (Hernández et al. 1995: 17). Per capita household income among Dominicans was substantially lower than the average for New York, $6,336 per person for Dominicans compared to an average of $16,412 for all New Yorkers (Ibid). The unemployment rate for Dominicans was close to double the rate for the overall New York City population (Ibid: 28).

Dominicans are doing worse than other immigrant groups as well. While the per capita income of the overall New York immigrant population grew by 16 percent over the last decade, Dominicans lagged behind with only a 7 percent increase (Ibid: 22). Dominicans are also more heavily concentrated in the lowest tiers of the labor market than other large Caribbean immigrant groups. In 1990 virtually one-half (49 percent) of all Dominicans in the New York labor force were employed as operatives, laborers, and personal service workers. The figures for Jamaicans, Haitians, and Cubans were 37 percent, 45 percent, and 40 percent, respectively. (Grasmuck and Pessar forthcoming).

What accounts for this poor performance? Clearly, the deterioration of New York's manufacturing and trade sectors has contributed to the lowering incomes and rising unemployment of Dominican workers. The growing Dominican economic enclave has turned out to be little more than a safety net for many workers. Yet, it is not economic hardship alone that accounts for the plight of many Dominican New Yorkers. Many carry social handicaps, such as low levels of education and membership in female-headed households, which further inhibit their prospects for advancement.

In 1990, more than 60 percent of Dominicans over 25 in New York City had not completed high school compared to 34 percent of Jamaicans, 35 percent of Haitians, and 53 percent of Cubans (Ibid). The impact of education on earnings becomes quite clear when we observe that Dominicans with less than high school education showed no improvement in their earnings (adjusted for inflation) during the '80s. By contrast, Dominican college graduates in New York earned 29 percent more in 1989 than 1979 (Hernández et al.: 39-40).[4]

There is a well-established link between female-headed households and poverty. Dominicans are no exception. Almost 40 percent of all Dominican households with children under the age of eighteen in New York City are female-headed and more than half (52 percent) of these are living below the poverty line (Ibid). This compares to only 19 percent of married Dominican householders living below the line. Dominican women face a substantial gender gap in earnings; while the annual earnings of Dominican male workers was $15,088, the comparable figure for women was only $11,347 (Hernández et al.: 49). Female-headed households are also more likely to be dependent on public assistance, another factor contributing to the high poverty rates of these households (Rosenbaum and Gilbertson 1995: 246).

Racial discrimination is yet another serious obstacle confronting Dominican immigrants. In the 1990 Census the vast majority of Dominicans in New York City identified themselves as either mulatto, specified as "other," (50 percent) or "black" (25 percent). Skin color is a very significant predictor of poverty among Dominicans with black and mulatto Dominicans having strikingly higher poverty levels than white Dominicans (Grasmuck and Pessar, forthcoming). Dominicans who are perceived as "white" by Caucasian Americans appear to enjoy a relative advantage in the labor market over darker-skinned workers. One fair-skinned Dominican woman explained, "When I got my job in the laundry, the owners said that even though I spoke Spanish, they would hire me because they didn't want any Blacks working for them." While she related this account with clear pride, the experience of racism has been denigrating and stinging for the majority of Dominicans who become the targets of discrimination. Consider the words of one dark-skinned Dominican:

> I was sitting in the waiting room of this big corporate office waiting for my interviewer to come out. A woman wandered out into the room I was sitting in, looked at me, looked around, and returned to her office. A few minutes later she did the same thing again. After the third time, she finally asked, "Are you Luis Rodríguez?" I replied, "Yes," as the woman tried to explain her way out of the blunder she had just made. "I was looking for someone who looked different, I mean Hispanic, I mean..." (Carter 1994:36).

The experience of being "confused" with African Americans and being discriminated against because of their dark pigmentation is especially unsettling for Dominican immigrants. They come from a society where to be partly white (the case for most Dominicans) is to be non-black. The racial category of black is largely reserved for the highly disdained Haitian immigrants and their descendants in the Dominican Republic. As social scientists, José del Castillo and Martin F. Murphy write:

> Throughout Dominican history, the elite ideology has defined the [D]ominican as a descendent of the Spanish and indigenous populations; the Dominican was considered a mestizo and when the color of his skin and other phenotypical characteristics of the African were noted, he was called a "blanco de la tierra," (white of the land). The Dominican systematically denied at the formal and official levels his African heritage and his condition as mulatto, to the extreme that officially and popularly he called himself "indio" (Indian).

His Haitian neighbors were the descendants of Africans, but not the Dominicans (1987: 51).

Racial issues will undoubtedly be salient for second-generation Dominicans who not only are exposed to alternative cultural constructions of race in the United States, but are also likely to experience both racial discrimination and racial pride in a different way than their parents. We see such signs of change emerging in the words of a second-generation Dominican college student who related her pride in being, in her words, "Afro-Caribbean." She told me that she challenges her mother's advice to call herself *blanca* (white), to revere her father's light-skinned, blue-eyed ancestors, and to minimize her mother's much darker-skinned forbearers. The politics of racial identity is, nonetheless, tricky. Some second-generation Dominicans, like one 22-year old male, feel ambivalent about identifying as Black, and instead come to emphasize their "Latino-ness:"

> All we see on television when we arrive is how bad blacks are, so we cling to our difference, our Latino-ness, in order to say we are not those blacks that you hear about in the streets or see on the news. We aren't bad. But at the same time, it feels ridiculous not to embrace our blackness because many dark Dominicans do live as other blacks, treated as blacks by white people, and other Latinos who act like there is one Latino phenotype, like there's a way to look Latino...I'm black and Latino, a black Latino—we exist, you know (Carter 1994: 28).

CONCLUSION

Most Dominicans come to New York in pursuit of economic advancement. There are some remarkable success stories, like Angel Lozano whose sales from his food processing plant reached $3.8 million in 1990 (Guarnizo 1992: 244). Indeed, the 92 firms included in Guarnizo's study had a net worth of approximately $35.5 million; and yielded some $4.4 million in income for their owners (Ibid: 204). Members of New York's Dominican middle class are justified in bristling against media portrayals that disregard the considerable diversity within the Dominican community and rush, instead, to proclaim Dominicans as the "losers" among new immigrant groups (Grasmuck and Pessar, forthcoming). Nonetheless, when we look at the population as a whole, key socio-economic indicators clearly point to the fact that Dominicans concentrate in the ranks of the city's "have-nots."

END NOTES

1. It should be noted that these labor force statistics include both persons actually employed at the time of the Census and the last job of those who were unemployed at the time of the interview.

2. While retail trade brings few rewards for *bodegueros* struggling in saturated markets, Guarnizo did find that among his respondents commerce held the greatest financial promise. Whereas the average income reported by the Dominican owners surveyed was $55,009, half the respondents who reported incomes of $75,000 operated commercial ventures (Guarnizo 1992: 222-223).

3. There is some controversy here. Guarnizo found that his 92 sampled firms paid an average hourly wage of $8.90, twice as high as the legal minimum wage. These salaries, however, did not include any type of fringe benefit. It is noteworthy that Guarnizo's findings are based on data gathered from employers, while the respondents in the other studies were Dominican workers.

4. Of those Dominicans who emigrated to the United States between the years 1985 and 1990, 11 percent were college graduates. This is up from an earlier figure of 5 percent for those Dominicans who emigrated during the prior two decades. Moreover, 27 percent of Dominicans born in the United States over the age of 25 are college graduates (Grasmuck and Pessar, forthcoming).

4

Dominican Immigrant Families: Continuity and Change

When Dominicans move to the United States, they attempt, in many ways, to reproduce the cultural landscape and lifeways of the country left behind. Inevitably, however, new or modified cultural and social forms are created in the new environment. These processes are clearly at work in the Dominican immigrant family, where members try to maintain key gender and generational norms at the same time as they modify certain social practices to accommodate to altered circumstances. In this chapter we explore how regular female employment forces Dominican family members to grapple with traditional, patriarchal values and norms, on the one hand, and newly emergent, more egalitarian patterns of authority and responsibility, on the other. We also consider how new opportunities available to Dominican youth have sometimes led to challenges to parental authority.

Before we begin, a cautionary note is in order. Just as there is tremendous variation among families in the United States—a fact which precludes any discussion of the typical "American family"—so there is much diversity and variation among Dominican families both in the Dominican Republic and the United States. Still, there are certain values, hierarchies of power, and social practices that are shared by many

Dominican families. It is these widely shared values, hierarchies, and practices that I describe, and the reader should bear in mind that they characterize many, but not all Dominican families.

DOMINICAN FAMILIES BACK HOME

Before they emigrated, most Dominican immigrants lived in a nuclear or extended-nuclear family, either as a child or as a member of a conjugal pair. A smaller number of immigrants resided in single parent or extended-single parent units (Grasmuck and Pessar 1991).

Nuclear families in the Dominican Republic are commonly quite patriarchal, with formal authority residing with the senior male. Publicly, at least, the image of the husband as the authority figure is maintained even though there are numerous, subtle ways that wives exercise a voice in, or sometimes veto, male decisions (Hendrick 1974). As patriarch, the man is expected to be the primary, if not sole, breadwinner, household head, and representative of the family in public life. In contrast, the woman's "place" is in the home, meeting the needs of the family. As one Dominican refrain expresses it, "el hombre en la calle y la mujer en el hogar" ("the man in the street and the woman in the home"). While this model of gender relations is predicated on a system of reciprocal exchanges between husband and wife, these exchanges are by no means equitable. Rather, men commonly enjoy a host of special privileges including far greater liberty to appropriate household income for their own use, to socialize outside of the home, and to form extramarital relations (Báez and Taulé 1993). As many of my female informants related, such male privilege could contribute to interpersonal and financial strains within families. Sometimes these pressures lead to marital disruptions. And, it is noteworthy that divorced and separated women are more likely to migrate to the United States (Gurak and Kritz 1987). Nonetheless, women are usually advised to avoid marital discord by reacting to husbands' excesses with patience and resignation. According to one expert on Dominican families, the ideology goes somewhat like this:

A woman has to marry; she marries, and marriage is like a lottery— you cannot predict what you will get. You cannot tell how a man will turn out. He may be a *gallero* (aficionado of cock fighting), a heavy drinker, or a womanizer. Whatever happens, it is the woman's duty to bear (literally, support) it all and remain faithful and responsible—remain that is, a 'serious woman'. If she behaves properly, as she should, one day her husband will stop his irresponsible behavior and dedicate himself to his wife" (Brown 1975: 325).

DOMINICAN IMMIGRANT FAMILIES

With Dominican settlement in New York, many couples have come to fashion a division of authority and responsibilities within the family that is somewhat more equitable. Changes have been most evident in three areas: beliefs about household authority, budgetary control, and the allocation of household members to housework tasks.

For most Dominicans the status of household head is equated with the role of breadwinner. According to a 1981 survey of Dominicans residing in New York, less than one-third (31 percent) of the women had been employed prior to emigration, whereas 92 percent worked for pay at some time since moving to the United States (Gurak and Kritz 1982). As Dominican immigrant women have come to demonstrate their capacity to share material responsibility with men on more or less equal terms, they have asserted the right to assume the status of household head alongside their husbands. Thus, in response to my questions, Who is the household head now? and, Who was the head previous to your emigration?, many echoed the words of this woman:

We both are the household heads. If both husband and wife are earning salaries then they should equally rule in the household. In the Dominican Republic it is always the husband who gives the orders in the household. But here when

the two are working, the woman feels herself the
equal of the man in ruling the home.

Household budgeting is another arena is which women
have sought and won greater equality. In interviews in the
early 1980s with immigrant women, I found that in the Dominican Republic prior to emigration, men generally controlled the budget in their households even though women
often contributed income on a regular or semi-regular basis.
Some households followed a traditional, patriarchal pattern
in which members gave all or part of their wages or profits to
the senior male who, in turn, oversaw the payment of household expenses. In others, the senior male amassed all of the
family income and then gave his wife an allowance to cover
such basic expenditures as food and clothing. In the United
States today far fewer Dominican households follow a male-
controlled pattern of budgeting. Indeed, pooling income is
now the dominant pattern. That is, the husband, wife, and
working children pool a specific amount of their wages or
profits for shared household expenses, such as food, rent, and
utilities. The rest of their income is usually divided between
joint or individual savings accounts and personal consumption items.

Thirty-three-year-old Carmen Rubio and her husband
Orlando, 38, explained to me how the transition from a male-
controlled form of budgeting to a pooled pattern occurred in
their household. Before emigrating in 1978 Carmen had been
a housewife. Orlando, then an accountant in a law office in
Santo Domingo, provided her with a weekly allowance for
the basics items. While they discussed major purchases such
as a new automobile, Orlando had the final say on all such expenditures.

Once in New York, it was decided that both would seek
employment: Carmen found work in a doll factory and Orlando worked as an accountant in a cousin's supermarket. In
Carmen's words, "At first I did what most women did back
home. I gave Orlando my pay check to use to pay the bills. He
gave me an allowance for food and other essentials." Some
months after their arrival Carmen needed a new dress for her
niece's wedding, and she asked Orlando for $100. He balked.

Carmen, smarting at his refusal, sought advice and help from her female relatives who had lived in New York for many years. It was actually Carmen's brother, a resident in the United States for six years, who intervened after hearing about the dispute. According to Carmen, "He told Orlando that as long as I was bringing in good money I had the right to buy what I wanted, as long as all the pressing bills were paid. He said that here couples put their wages together and shared in paying bills."

For his part, Orlando explained that at the time of the dispute he did not want Carmen to buy such an expensive dress, because they had many debts to repay linked to their emigration. Nonetheless, he recanted, "They told me I was being old-fashioned and not appreciative of Carmen's help. They also told me that women have many more expenses here than at home, like clothes to wear to work. I could see that here, honorable men, like my brother-in-law, were handling affairs differently than they did back home; so I decided I could change too." Significantly, both Carmen and Orlando now claim that they like the pooled pattern of budgeting better than the household allowance mode. "We each know how much the other earns and we discuss how our money is being spent and saved," Orlando explained. "Back home Carmen would sometimes accuse me of spending my money on vices, like gambling, while she struggled to feed the family. I would tell her she was wrong; my earnings just didn't go as far as they did in the past. Now she sees my pay check; there are no secrets. It's better."

Consistent with research on other working-class families (Hood 1983; Lamphere et al. 1993), I found that many Dominican immigrant women were able to use their wage-earning as leverage to obtain assistance from husbands in housework and child care. In a sense, Dominican women are simply following the logic of what one writer calls the "marketwork/housework bargain" (Hood 1983). An underlying assumption in this "bargain" is that men's principal responsibility is to provide for the family's economic needs, the woman's is to maintain the household. However, if the woman assumes economic responsibility for the family by engaging in wage work, as many Dominican immigrant women have done, then the allocation of other household responsibilities should change as well.

The vast majority of Dominican women and men I met in New York believed that when both partners worked outside the home, the husband should "help" with tasks such as shopping, washing dishes, and child care. Occasionally, they even cook, as in the case of Ernesto Collado, a chef in New York, who assumed that his contribution to running the household should include cooking at home as well. When I visited the Collado apartment, I found Ernesto preparing dinner. He said he would never have been found in the kitchen, let alone cooking, in the Dominican Republic. There, he told me, the kitchen was solely the women's domain—"la cocina se respeta." Yet, on the island, his wife would not be working outside the house; he alone would be the breadwinner. Once both he and his wife were working, they realized that "if both worked outside the house, both should work inside as well. Now that we are in the United States, we should adopt American ways."

There seems to be a direct relationship between the amount of money a woman contributes to the household and the degree to which her spouse is willing or feels compelled to engage in domestic responsibilities. Dominican women who contribute almost half, if not more, to the household budget can usually depend on greater male involvement in domestic tasks than women who make more modest financial contributions. This was the case for Ismelda Nuñez, who explained that when her children were very young she worked a few hours a day at home sewing for a neighborhood garment factory (i.e., industrial homework). "I worked fewer hours than my husband and I wasn't bringing in much money. If he decided to help me bathe the children or do the dishes, that was fine; but I never insisted, not then." Once the children were older and in school, Ismelda began working full-time in a shoe factory. "I work nine or ten hours a day," she stated. "I am bringing in a lot of money to help my husband.... He actually does things around the house now without my even asking."

Many of the women I spoke to indicated that they did not explicitly request that their husbands assist them in household labors. Rather, many said, "the changes just happened." Often they were the result of expediency. For example, Ernesto Collado first began cooking for the family when his work schedule permitted him to return home before his wife. "I opened the door on three kids complaining that their school lunch was lousy. They knew I was a chef so they kind of insisted that I start dinner."

Dominican women consistently mentioned male assistance in housework and child care when they compared their life in the United States favorably with that in the Dominican Republic. Yet none of my informants went so far as to suggest that men could or should act as women's equals in the domestic sphere. Indeed, the following woman's words capture the belief of most of the working women I spoke to: "I know of cases where the man assumes the housekeeping and child care responsibilities. But I don't believe a man can be as good as a woman; she is made for the home and the man is made to work."

Such sentiments suggest that women's wage work may have led to greater changes in domestic social practice than in actual gender ideology and norms. On this score the rhetoric with which Dominican women describe changes in traditional gender relations is telling. I often heard women comment favorably on the increased sharing and unity (*unión*) between husbands and wives that wage earning and residence in the United States afforded. In particular, they praised husbands for "helping" their wives in child care and housework. By contrast, women usually described their own wage-earning as "helping" their husbands. In my opinion, both sets of comments reflect women's attempts to reconcile wage work and the changes in domestic life it has occasioned on the one hand, with a more paramount set of enduring values on the other. Despite the acknowledgment that, while in the United States, women may need "to help" husbands earn a livelihood and husbands may legitimately be called upon "to help" working women at home, a more conservative message about the sexes is implied. It is the same message we noted in our earlier discussion of pre-migration families. It holds that women are persons whose primary interests and responsibilities are rooted in the home, while men are beings who are responsible for maintaining the family by their labors in the workplace. The contours of the wage-working and domestic lives of the two Dominican women profiled below, illustrate the resiliency of this dichotomous construct.

Marta Torres, a young wife and mother of three young children turned to sewing at home to resolve the pull between her domestic obligations and the pressing financial needs of her family. She had worked previously in a garment shop where she had been employed since the age of 16. "My mother lived nearby," she explained, "and when my first two babies were born, she used to take care of them in her apartment; I'd pick them up each evening when I returned from work." Marta's mother cared for the children until her own husband was laid-off and she was forced to find a job. No other relative was available for child care and Marta did not want to entrust her young children to the care of a stranger.

The possibility existed for Marta's husband, Wilfredo, to assume the bulk of the child care, since he was a chef's assistant in a restaurant and often worked the late shift. While the couple had discussed the possibility of Wilfredo's arranging a permanent slot on the night shift, they quickly rejected the idea. "Neither Wilfredo nor I liked the idea. We were both raised with the belief that the woman's place is in the home. In the early years, especially, the children need the warmth of their mother," Marta told me. Eventually, it was decided that Wilfredo would find a second job, instead. Marta insisted on "helping" Wilfredo since she was concerned that even with his two jobs, the couple would not be able to save the money needed to send their oldest to parochial school the following year. She managed to set aside these savings by arranging to sew garments at home while the children were sleeping or watching television. This "compromise" exacted a price on both Marta and Wilfredo. Exhausted from holding down two jobs, Wilfredo ceased to help in child care and housework, activities he had participated in to a limited extent when both spouses were employed full-time. Marta, too, felt overburdened; she now did all the domestic work and combined this with industrial homework when she had brief breaks from her domestic responsibilities.

Marta readily conceded that she missed the companionship of her co-workers and the assistance in domestic tasks previously extended by her husband and mother. Nonetheless, she stated, "A woman's first obligation is to her husband and her children. When the children are older I'll go back to work full-time; now my place is at home."

The notion of a working wife "helping" her husband becomes even more problematic in cases when the woman's wages are no longer necessary to maintain a comfortable standard of living in the United States. In these circumstances, women's continued wage work does more than challenge the ideal of the sole male breadwinner; it also contradicts the common practice of marking a Dominican family's elevated social status by confining the woman to the domestic sphere. In many instances, Dominican women have chosen to place immigrant ideology (with its stress on social advancement), traditional family ideology, and the ideal of the sole male provider, before the personal gains that wage work has brought them. Witness the following example.

Prior to moving to New York in 1968, Margarita Ramírez was a housewife and her husband, Roque, was employed in his father's supermarket. Upon arriving in New York, Margarita immediately found a job in a fairly large, unionized shop in New York's garment district. Roque began working as a dishwasher in a restaurant, soon advanced to the ranks of chief chef, and finally left after he was able to afford his own small grocery store.

Over the years Margarita insisted on working despite Roque's persistent protests. She did so in order to have enough money to buy a home in New York, send the children to parochial school, and purchase a small business. Once they had achieved these goals, however, Roque redoubled his appeal that Margarita cease working outside the home. Margarita recalled, "He said it would be good for the children and good for all of us. At first I protested, because I never again wanted to be totally dependent upon a man. I feared that he would start saying the money that entered the house was his alone. I worried that he would start using this money for bad things, like alcohol, heavy gambling, and women....At that time we pooled our wages and what was his was mine and vice versa. We had built so much union and I feared it would all disappear. You see when I worked we were partners struggling together for our family's advancement (*progreso*)."

Ultimately, Margarita accepted the decision to stop working for wages. "I began to think about how much I had suffered in this country to make something for my family. And I thought, even though we own a home and a business, most Americans think the worst of us. They think we all sell drugs, have too many babies, take away their jobs, or are living off the government (i.e., receiving welfare). I decided, I'm going to show them that I am as good as they are, that my husband is so successful that I don't have to work at all....So I risked the union that Roque and I had established through both of us working and struggling together. I did it; I sacrificed for the good of our reputation as a family. You could say we have a different kind of union now, one under the leadership of a hardworking and successful *jefe de la casa* (man of the house).

DISBANDED UNIONS

Women's employment and their major contribution to household budgets have promoted greater gender parity within many Dominican households. Some, like Marta and Margarita, have sacrificed these gains, however, in the name of powerful gender constructs that identify women foremost with the domestic sphere. Still others have seen their struggles to attain more equitable domestic relations and social mobility end in dismantled unions and poverty. Of the fifty-five women I interviewed extensively in New York, eighteen have divorced or separated from a partner while in the United States. Fourteen cited a struggle over domestic authority and social practices as the primary disruptive factor.

Sometimes difficulties arose when the woman lived and worked in the United States prior to sponsoring her mate's migration. Women reported that newly-arrived husbands typically became unnerved by what they viewed as an inversion of gender roles. While many men adamantly insisted that their wives return to a more traditional pattern of household authority and budgeting, a few reacted quite differently.

Claiming that their wives were trying to wear the pants in the family, these men insisted upon their wives becoming true ("male") breadwinners by assuming responsibility for major fixed expenses, such as food and housing. For several women the breaking point came when the man monopolized his salary for personal expenses, such as entertainment, while at the same time demanding a disproportionate economic contribution from his wife.

Clara Duarte, who sponsored her husband's emigration after residing in New York without him for three years, described several bitter and humiliating fights over the control and allocation of money. When Mario first arrived in New York, he insisted that she hand her pay check over to him; she refused. He then demanded that she continue to pay the rent and utilities, "since the contracts were solely in her name." At first Clara agreed to cover the major household expenses, figuring that she would give Mario a chance both to find a relatively well-paying job and to learn how other Dominican immigrant couples managed household budgeting. "But, still, after two years, he continued to use his money for his philandering and claim he didn't have enough to pay our bills," Clara explained. "I saw he would never change. I was still young, we had no children, and I figured I could find another man who was more understanding, a better companion." Clara was fortunate to find such a partner a few years after she divorced Mario. Her new husband was a Dominican who arrived in the United States as a youngster. Juan had seen his own parents jointly manage the household budget, and he readily adopted this pattern when he and Clara married.

While some of my married informants were fortunate enough to emigrate to the United States together, most endured several years of separation prior to their reunion in New York. During these prolonged absences, suspicions or actual instances of marital infidelity proved common and were a source of tension for many couples. When I first met Julia Torres in the Dominican Republic, she was eager to be reunited with her husband, Eusebio, who had departed for New York five years earlier, soon after their wedding. As I helped Julia fill out forms for her U.S. visa, she confided about rumors concerning Eusebio's affair with a Puerto Rican woman.

Some years later we met again, this time in her sister's Washington Heights apartment. With great passion, Julia recounted that when she and Eusebio were finally reunited, she found that the rumors were true.

> I told him, very calmly, that I could understand why a man who was on his own might need the warmth of another woman. But I told him that now his wife was here, and he had to choose between an adulteress and me. His mother joined me and called him all kinds of names. But he had had a son with the Puerto Rican slut and she had control over him.

At first Eusebio repented and agreed to establish a household with Julia. The arrangement was short-lived. Soon Julia heard disturbing rumors again of Eusebio's continuing affair with his Puerto Rican lover. Julia packed up her belongings and moved in with her sister. When we discussed Eusebio's affair and her decision to disband the union, Julia observed that she was pleasantly surprised that none of her family members advised her to aguantar and wait patiently for Eusebio to mend his ways. In fact, both her sister and Eusebio's mother advised her to first look for a job to support herself and then seek another, more suitable mate.

Prolonged male unemployment, combined with men's insistence on maintaining the perks of male privilege in the household, can also lead to marital discord, as the following case illustrates. In 1980, Oscar Rosario lost his job in the shipping department of a belt factory that had relocated to Florida. Due to his undocumented status, Oscar was afraid to apply for unemployment benefits and as a consequence all financial responsibilities for the five-member Rosario family fell on his wife's shoulders. Mercedes worked in a lamp factory by day and sold Avon products at night and over the weekends in her neighborhood. Although Oscar had thought it would be easy to find a new job, he spent several months in a fruitless search and then became despondent. According to

Mercedes, during this time "He didn't lift a finger to help me around the house. No, he only sulked and did nothing. A neighbor of mine told me I was crazy for supporting him while he did nothing." Nonetheless, she continued to accept his behavior until "he started to waste the money I slaved for, drinking and staying out later and later with his friends instead of helping me at night. I told him to get out and only come back when he could contribute like a man to the family." After months of bitter fighting, Oscar agreed to move in with his mother. In his absence, Mercedes convinced her newly-arrived cousin to move in with her. According to Mercedes, the cousin has provided her with companionship, help with household expenses, and assistance in child care.

Some unions foundered in the wake of men's confusion and anger over their appropriate status and responsibilities when female partners acquired welfare payments. Some men felt that their principal role as provider had been usurped by the woman with the help of a more powerful patron, the State. Moreover, some resented the control and independence welfare benefits gave their partner.

> "With that money from the government she thought she was mighty big," one divorced man said. "She started thinking that she could manage without me.... Even though she was home all day she did things like telling me to mind the children and wash the dishes.... So I stopped bringing my money home; I kept it all in my own bank account. I thought, let her use her money from her new patron to pay for the rent, food, and clothing."

The tension created in marriages over the woman's receipt of welfare benefits is part of a larger configuration that finds Dominican female immigrants increasing their control over an array of societal resources, while Dominican men see their control over social and economic resources actually diminish.

As these case studies show, immigrant life in the United States equips Dominican women with new material, social, and cultural resources. These resources empower some women to make more demands upon their husbands and to be willing to disband unions in which husbands refuse to compensate them, even minimally, for their involvement in traditional male activities, such as wage-earning. Sadly though, women's empowerment often carries a price. When household bonds are severed, the goal of the migration project—social advancement for the family—often falters, because the individual resources of single members, especially women, are insufficient to sustain it. The newfound autonomy of many immigrant women may, in the end, lead to poverty.

Such was the case for Altagracia Ortiz, who emigrated to New York from Santiago in 1971 at the age of 26, leaving behind her husband and children with his parents. An accomplished seamstress, Altagracia easily found work through a cousin in a unionized apparel factory. By 1977 she had enough money to successfully sponsor her husband Carlito's migration.

The couple's problems began almost from the moment Carlito stepped off the plane. "Maybe I had changed after so many years of being on my own, being my own boss," she stated. "When I left [the Dominican Republic,] I was an innocent who was totally dependent on her husband's wages. Here it was different and he couldn't stomach it."

Altagracia said that she and her husband struggled constantly over household budgeting and socializing. "He wanted me to give him my salary and then he would give me a small household allowance. I knew he would use my hardearned money for heavy drinking and who knows what else. I insisted that we pool our wages and decide together on all household expenses.... He would get furious when I used some of my money to go out with some girl friends, but he saw nothing wrong with staying out all night with some of his friends."

The breaking point came when Carlito had trouble finding a job, a few years after they had brought their children to New York. Yet he refused "to help me with the housework and children, even though he was staying home and sleeping the whole day. So finally I said to him, 'you are no man. You want me to be both *el jefe de casa* (male household head) and *la ama de casa* (housewife).' I told him to move in with his sister and he did; our marriage of more than twenty-five years was over.... Maybe if he had tried harder to find work, or maybe if he had tried to help even a little, we would still be together. But, imagine, he just refused to help."

Altagracia was acutely aware of the social and economic ramifications her decision to disband the union entailed. She explained, "In my country all little girls, no matter how rich or poor they may be, dream of a church wedding with the bride all dressed in white lace. This means the girl has respect and social standing. She is not like the woman who lives without a man and has children with whomever—like they say in my country 'one poor hen with lots of chicks all fathered by different roosters!' So here I was after so much struggling to have that church wedding, to bring my family together in New York, only to be a women left alone without a husband....It was one of the saddest days in my life. Not only did I lose the respect I once had as a married woman, but my children and I lost the material support Carlito was able to provide. And here we are today *pobrecitos* ("poor little ones"), as you can see."

Altagracia's situation worsened when only five months after her separation, she was permanently laid-off from her long-standing job at the apparel factory. After experiencing problems both in gaining another job through the union and in obtaining unemployment benefits, Altagracia decided to apply for welfare. She combined this income with wages she received, "working off the books" in a neighborhood sweatshop. In 1983 Altagracia received an average weekly wage of $80 plus $135 in welfare. This allowed her to pay the rent on the apartment she shared with her children and to afford only the most basic necessities.

"Somos una familia unida" ("We are a united family") many Dominicans say with pride. This is the ideal image of the family where balanced reciprocity between the sexes purportedly exists and the common good comes before self interest. Yet, in practice this is a family model in which patriarchal authority and male privilege often predominate. Migration provides social and economic resources that permit women greater authority in the household and support challenges to male privilege when it jeopardizes the collective good of the family. For the most part, however, Dominican immigrant women have only nibbled at the edges of patriarchy, as evidenced by their discourse (i.e., "helping" husbands financially) and by their willingness to abandon personal gains when domestic needs and social advancement beckon. Unfortunately, the U.S. labor market is also organized on the principle that women's wages are supplemental. As a consequence, many working women, like Altagracia, who head their households are reduced to poverty.

DOMINICAN YOUTH: CHALLENGES TO GENERATIONAL HIERARCHY

It is not only women who have gained access to new social and economic resources with which to challenge male authority in the family. Dominican immigrant children have also taken on responsibilities and entered into social spheres previously controlled foremost by their fathers and secondarily by their mothers. In this process, fathers in particular have seen an erosion of their elevated status. Moreover, many men fear that they have lost the absolute respect of their children—traditionally the prerogative of the authoritarian Dominican father (Hendricks 1974).

In the Dominican Republic, it was the male household head who was primarily responsible for acting as liaison between the family and those external social institutions that contained resources critical to its well-being. In the United States, by contrast, it is often immigrant children who have emerged as intermediaries, owing to their greater English-language proficiency and familiarity with U.S. bureaucracies. This not only inverts traditional generational lines of expertise and privileged access to important resources, it also creates a situation ripe for manipulation as children are called upon to interpret the outside world for their elders.

The experiences of the Peña family illustrate several of these quandaries. Back in the Dominican Republic, Máximo Peña, was the undisputed liaison between his family and the wider society. For example, he alone transacted with Dominican government officials to obtain the proper documentation needed to emigrate to the United States. Yet, when he and his wife emigrated to New York in 1978, they first had to call upon trusted relatives who had lived in the United States for several years to assume this role of culture broker. Over the years, though, it has been the Peña children who have learned English fluently and mastered the intricacies of U.S. bureaucracies. As a result, fourteen-year-old Denise translates the monthly bills and helps her parents fill out the forms; she also brokered recently for her father when he applied for disability benefits. Denise admitted to me that she felt pride in being able to help her parents "after all they have sacrificed to make us a life here." Nonetheless, she was also embarrassed at being given so much responsibility at such a young age. Denise's father, too, lamented that he had to rely so extensively on his children due to his limited English-language proficiency. He added, however: "I have raised my children to be honorable and respectful. They never deceive us. I know of other children who lie to their parents. Like they tell them a phone bill is for $100, when it really is $70. And then the child pays the bill and pockets the extra $30." While a few other informants related cases in which children abused their role as intermediaries, the most commonly voiced concern I heard involved a diminution of the fathers' authority; "It's a real pride check [to our parents]," as one young man observed.

Many Dominican adults fault U.S. institutions, such as schools, child welfare agencies, and the police, for undermining the rights of parents to control and discipline their children. U.S. notions of child abuse and official measures to prevent it are particularly confusing and nettlesome for many Dominican parents. In one rather egregious case, a divorced mother was jailed for several days and her twelve-year-old daughter sent to a foster home after the mother was accused of child abuse by a school guidance counsellor. The counsellor had apparently questioned the girl about a welt on her face and had called in authorities when the youngster admitted that her mother had beaten her. Several years after this incident, Rosa Cepeda, the girl's mother, explained to me that she had hit her daughter across the face after learning from a neighbor that the girl had not returned directly home after school, as expected, but had spent many hours unchaperoned at the home of her boyfriend. Rosa stated:

> She knows I am at work during the day and cannot check on her. And she took advantage of my trust and my absence. If I had not hit her, she would have lost all respect for me. Dominicans expect their parents to be forceful. If I had not struck her, they [her neighbors] would have said, "That girl has no father; and her mother has no control over that one. She will end up on the streets alone.

Rosa was deeply embarrassed and angered by her imprisonment. But she railed most vociferously against a child welfare system that had placed her daughter in a foster home, then took no action after the girl ran away and lived on the streets for three months without Rosa's knowledge.

While an extreme case, Rosa's experience points up several factors that have eroded certain immigrant parents' authority and control over their children. First, many parents work very long hours, and this undermines their ability to supervise their children. This is especially grave when there is only one adult available within a household. Second, the cultural beliefs and norms regarding the discipline of children are clearly different in the Dominican and U.S. contexts. As the above case illustrates, the public disciplining of daughters is especially important for those Dominicans who insist that propriety and chastity are interlinked and that both communicate the respectability of the girl's family and her suitability as a good wife. It should be added that children are often the agents who communicate information about child abuse laws to their parents—a situation that is ripe for miscommunication and distortion. As Luis Guarnizo writes:

> Misleading perceptions of what constitutes child abuse make parents afraid of chastising their children for fear of being deported if they were ever accused of abuse. As one parent put it, "Here one cannot even scold one's own children because

they'll go and accuse you of child abuse" (forth-coming: 33).

Indeed, a frustrated father, who complained of his rebel-lious son's threats to call the police, told me: "There is no re-spect for the father in this country. Back home, just let my son pick up the phone and call the police. Let them come. It wouldn't matter. There they know it is the father who has the ultimate authority." He was so distressed about the erosion of parental control that he sent his son back to the Dominican Republic to be cared for by the youth's "old-fashioned" grandparents.

While many families send children with behavioral prob-lems back home to the island, others in the United States wait for years to be finally reunited with children who have been reared by family members in the Dominican Republic. Many such parents shared with me the fear that after so many years of separation, their children would no longer respect them. Having lived apart from his two sons for over a decade, Ernesto Duarte worried, "When I left they were babies. Now they're almost men. They have only known me as the father who sends dollars so they can eat and be clothed. I have not been there to gain their love and respect." When Ernesto was finally reunited with his sons, he encountered two youths who were extremely formal and distant. They turned more to their mother, Carmen, for support and guidance, perhaps be-cause she had traveled yearly to the Dominican Republic to spend summers with them. Carmen considered the family fortunate. She told me of other children who arrived in New York after years of separation from their parents and strug-gled to make a healthy adjustment. Carmen and many other Dominicans I spoke to attributed the rebelliousness and anti-social behaviour of certain Dominican youth to prolonged family separation.

Tensions between the generations also emerge over chil-dren's socializing outside the home. To their children's cha-grin, many of my informants only permitted their children to go to social clubs, dances, and the movies if a trusted adult went along as chaperone. Adults view this vigilance as an at-tempt to shelter their children from the scourges of crime, violence, and drugs. This is certainly sufficient justification for this supervision. Yet there is likely to be more behind this parental monitoring. Consider the words of a Dominican social worker who concluded her comments about parental supervision with the observation that Dominican youth are kept virtual prisoners in their homes, and "parents are terrified about the loss of control over their children." It seems likely that the assiduous attempts of parents to monitor children's movements outside the home is one way in which immigrant parents attempt to reclaim some degree of control over children whose knowledge of English and access to U.S. institutions have come to challenge traditional lines of parental privilege and authority.

While parents express fears about the perils of street life for both sons and daughters, a double standard often operates with sons being given more liberty than daughters to socialize without direct parental supervision. Several working daughters I knew faced strong pressure from peers to socialize outside of the family context—and they had the financial means to do so. Yet these young women found themselves severely constrained by parents who continue to equate "good families" with highly protected and disciplined daughters. Daughters sometimes channel their resentment of over-protective parents into their studies. Their goal is to leave home after high school and attend a distant university. Others, like seventeen-year-old María, enter into an early marriage to escape parental vigilance. As she explained, "My father always bugged me about my going out with boys and I could never do anything. By being married, I can do more things now without him worrying if I will remain a young lady [virgin]" (cited in Hendricks 1974: 100).

Employment opportunities and earning power in New York for Dominican youth tend to be greater than in the Dominican Republic. This situation also bolsters their demands for more autonomy and independence. Employed children who are generous in giving their parents some of their earnings can help maintain the idealized notion of a unified Dominican family whose members contribute to a collective family budget. Yet when children contribute sizeable amounts to the family income they are also able to challenge more effectively parental control over their actions. This challenge has been felt more fully in New York than in the Dominican Republic owing both to children's greater earning power and to the fact that Dominican youth are exposed in the schools and in the media to American values of individualism and independence. Such was the case with Ricardo, an eighteen- year-old delivery boy. Ricardo's father objected to his son's dropping out of high school before graduation and tried to persuade him to return. Ricardo stated,

> "Back home I would have had to obey my father no matter what I thought, because I would have had no job and no money. Here I help him out. I still owe him respect as my father, but he kind of has to respect more what I think and do. He knows that if I get angry, I'll just leave and get myself my own apartment. Then it would be harder for him."

While employment does permit some youth, like Ricardo, to challenge their parents' wishes regarding schooling, other young Dominicans react very differently to their parents' stress on education. Many parents describe their own emigration as an act of sacrifice (*sacrificio*) taken on behalf of their children. Parents explain that they are willing to work in menial jobs to permit their children to acquire higher education in the United States, so "they will become professionals." One Dominican high school student who sought my help in identifying "good universities" for him, explained the pressure he felt to succeed.

> "I try to avoid hanging out with my friends so that I can get my studying done. My mother works so hard; it makes me feel bad. I'd like to get a job after school. But she tells me my job is to study, so that some day she can retire and I can support her with my salary as a doctor or lawyer."

Not surprisingly, Dominican parents take great pride in, and identify with, their educated childrens' achievements.

For example, Zelda, an apparel worker, explained that one son was going to be an historian and the other a philosopher. She then added, "And do you know what I am going to be? I am going to be all of this, because little by little I will be picking up something from each of them and from their friends. I will be listening and learning."

CONCLUSION

Dominican men have been heard to lament, "The Dominican Republic is a country for men; the United States is a country for women." Similarly parents complain of children who have become "Americanized," and thus challenge strict parental control to an extent unheard of back home. Both sets of concerns represent very real changes in both women's and children's access to social and economic resources—assets which in the past had securely buttressed patriarchy and parental control. Yet despite these changes, few wives or children have used their newfound power to completely reject these hierarchical structures. In fact, the endurance of traditional gender and generational patterns is striking. We see this endurance in the words and practices of many working women who diminish their contributions to their families and insist that they are simply "helping their husbands." We see it in the actions of dutiful sons who study for the future well-being of their parents. And we see it in the actions of daughters, who rather than truly challenging the ways in which gender and generation converge in Dominican families to limit their autonomy, seek higher education or early marriage as ways to escape parental vigilance and control. Yet, as we shall see in the next chapter, for some Dominican males even a modest erosion in their singular authority and control of the household has proved sufficiently unsettling to cause them to orchestrate a speedy return to the Dominican Republic.

5

Forging Lives "Aquí" [Here] and "Allá" [There]

The longing to return to the home country versus the pressures and incentives to settle here is a tension that most newcomers to the United States have confronted. Most have been forced to resolve this tension, and the majority have chosen to make a home here. Contemporary immigrants, however, have tended to be less inclined and less pressured to choose. The ability of immigrants, like Dominicans, to maintain a foothold in both societies is facilitated by several factors.

First, new immigrants benefit from recent revolutions in global transportation, communication, and technology. News of current events in the Dominican Republic are easily accessible to the immigrant in New York. It merely requires a walk to the corner newsstand, a flick of the radio or television dial to a Spanish-language station, or the placement of an overseas call. Family rites of passage, such as marriages and baptisms, are videoed and circulated between New York and the Dominican Republic. And electronic media help Dominican entrepreneurs manage businesses back home while they continue to reside in New York. Such flows of information, technology, social life, and finance make it difficult to know where the Dominican Republic ends and Dominican New York begins. According to the theories of transnationalism and global culture, this is how it should be. For, today's diaspora populations "imagine" and negotiate worlds where national boundaries, national cultures, and national identities are far less constraining and socially binding than was the case for earlier immigrant groups (see, Featherstone 1990; Basch et al. 1994).

Second, while earlier immigrant populations were pressured to discard ethnic identities, beliefs, and practices in order to assimilate into American society, post-1965 immigrants have entered a United States that is more tolerant of ethnic pluralism and multiculturalism. Dominicans have been elected and appointed to political offices in New York, and neighborhood schools and churches have been renamed to recognize Dominican heroes and saints. Dominican educators have grown in number and visibility in academic institutions ranging from elementary schools to universities, and they have insisted that Dominican history, social issues, and scholarship be added to the curriculum.[1] In these times of multiculturalism, Dominican New Yorkers selectively retain, appropriate, and refashion elements of both (island) Dominican and U.S. culture and society.

Third, contemporary immigrants face economies at home and abroad which are characterized by both opportunity and uncertainty. Many choose to hedge their bets by participating in both economies. Indeed, as we shall see, some Dominican entrepreneurs effectively link businesses in New York with enterprises on the island. Fourth, labor-exporting nations increasingly acknowledge the fact that members of their diaspora communities are important resources which should not be lost to the national polity and society. Jamaica, for example, is one such nation that permits dual citizenship. Dominican legislators are currently designing policies to facilitate the greater participation of immigrants in the political and economic affairs of the island republic. Fifth, many new immigrants are "people of color." As such, they face the real prospect of having their educational and economic achievements dismissed or devalued by representatives of white, mainstream America. Thus, many immigrants retain contacts with a home society whose members, they hope, will value the sacrifices and achievements made by compatriots abroad.

This final chapter considers the loyalties and deep ties that many Dominican New Yorkers maintain with the Dominican Republic. It also reexamines the ways in which Dominicans are forging a place for themselves as a significant ethnic group within New York. While these two orientations to New York and to the Dominican Republic, may seem opposed and contradictory, they are actually complementary. Dominican immigrants are successfully constructing transnationalized lives. Some Dominicans do return to the Dominican Republic, and the chapter discusses the phenomenon of return migration, beginning with an an exploration of Dominican women's and men's contrasting orientations to return. This is followed by an examination of the many challenges returnees face in their quest for full and equitable reincorporation into Dominican society. The chapter concludes with a discussion of the difficulties Dominican New Yorkers and *retornados* (returnees) face in exacting appropriate recognition and respect from elite circles in both the United States and the Dominican Republic.

NEW YORK AS A WAITING ROOM

To many Dominican New Yorkers, New York is a temporary way station, "a waiting room" rather than "a home" (Torres-Saillant 1989: 23). Torres-Saillant claims that the reluctance of his fellow Dominicans "to accept the finality of their settlement on this North American soil" has impeded the community's social advancement (Ibid: 14). He acknowledges that alienation from the host society is inherent in the very nature of being an immigrant; in the case of Dominicans, this alienation is exacerbated by their being poor newcomers in a city whose economy, housing stock, and public services have markedly deteriorated. Yet, he is also critical of the Dominican ethnic community's transient mentality and nostalgia for home. Of course reminders of home are all around. The newcomer's Dominican neighbors fill tenement halls with the sounds and the smells of the island. Dominican merchants "stimulate consumption by selling the past"(Ibid), as bodega owners stock shelves with brand-name commodities from the island and induce walk-in customers by blaring merengue rhythms into the street. And Washington-Heights medical clinics advertise a Dominican obstetrician on their staff, mindful of the market value held in the promise that new babies will be delivered into trusted, Dominican hands, if not actually upon Dominican soil. For their part, Dominican associations tend to focus more on life *allá* (there) than *aquí* (here). Numerous organizations are dedicated to sending funds back to members' home communities, and clubs are organized to promote Dominican culture and sports. In 1989, Torres-Saillant wrote:

> I know of not one of these organizations which purports to serve as channel for the newcomer to learn the ropes that will make the larger society accessible to him or her. On the contrary, for the most part these organizations serve instead as a kind of refuge from the stress of the mainstream (1989: 16).

Political activities in the New York Dominican community can also encourage transience, for they often suggest that Dominicans are first and foremost island citizens whose loyalties and destiny ought to remain firmly tied to their country of birth. Indeed, observers of political life among Dominicans in New York have noted that the majority remain more interested in, and committed to, political events in the Dominican Republic than to local politics (Georges 1984; Goris-Rosario 1994). In the late 1970s, for example, the main goal of the National Association of Dominicans Abroad (ANDE), was the right for Dominican immigrants to vote by absentee ballot in Dominican national and local elections (Georges 1984). All the major political parties of the Dominican Republic have offices in New York; and New York is one of the main fund-raising and campaign grounds for Dominican politicians. In 1990, approximately 20,000 Dominicans returned to the Dominican Republic to vote (Goris-Rosario 1991). Moreover, it is not uncommon to find wealthy Dominicans who have amassed fortunes in New York using their financial power to obtain diplomatic positions in such organizations as the Dominican Consulate in New York and the

Dominican Mission to the United Nations (Torres-Saillant 1989: 21).

This island orientation weighs heavily in Dominicans' comparatively low rate of naturalization as compared to other "new immigrants." According to the 1990 Census, 18 percent of all Dominican immigrants residing in the United States had naturalized. By contrast, immigrants from many Asian countries had naturalization rates well above 50 percent (Warren 1988:4). Among Dominican-born residents in New York City, 22 percent were U.S. citizens. This is one of the lowest rates of all Caribbean immigrants in New York City (Grasmuck and Pessar, forthcoming). Critics of the Dominican-centered, political culture in New York contend that it "contributes tremendously to keeping this community mentally distant from their immediate socio-economic and political reality" (Torres-Saillant 1989:21).

FROM IMMIGRANTS TO ETHNICS

Although a transient mentality remains pervasive, there are also clear signs that the Dominican community is emerging as a distinct ethnic group—one, moreover, that is disposed to make demands for recognition based on its significant presence.

The successful compaign to redraw district lines in Washington Heights (District 10) is a striking example of the "coming of age" of Dominican community associations and of the collaboration between Dominicans and other area Latinos.[2] The redistricting was a by-product of federal legislation directed at redressing the old practice of dividing geographic concentrations of ethnic groups into many districts to dilute their political influence. In New York City, as elsewhere in the United States, representatives of racial and ethnic minorities came forth to propose alternative plans for electoral districts in the hopes of eradicating such disenfranchisement. In redistricting hearings held in Northern Manhattan, members of Latino organizations, such as the Latino Voting Rights Committee, and predominately Dominican organizations, like the North Manhattan Committee for Fair Representation, argued for the legal recognition of District 10 as "a Dominican district." The proponents for redistricting pointed to the tremendous concentration of Dominicans in Washington Heights as well as their political cohesion. As evidence of this solidarity, they noted the great strides Dominicans had made in local School Board elections. They also argued that Dominicans led all other groups in investment in the local economy and thus deserved the just rewards of fair representation. In the words of the framers of one proposal for redistricting,

> Our merchants and entrepreneurs continue to contribute to the city and [s]tate's enrichment by paying sales, corporate, liability, property, insurance, FICA, unemployment and other taxes. In addition, and more importantly, are the jobs created by [our] vibrant economy. [It is an] economy that has kept this community alive and will continue to make it flourish for many more years to come (Hernández and Lescaille 1991: 5).

The proponents' arguments and their political organizing proved compelling; the lines of District 10 were reconfigured to reflect its Dominican majority and to create a district in which Dominican officials might be more readily elected. Subsequently, in the 1991 elections, Dominicans comprised the majority of the candidates who ran for the district's seat in the New York City Council. Guillermo Linares, who it will be recalled helped launch the movement for greater control over the neighborhood's schools, was elected as the first Dominican City Councilman.

TRANSNATIONAL LIVES: MAINTAINING A PRESENCE IN BOTH NEW YORK AND THE DOMINICAN REPUBLIC

According to conventional notions of assimilation, this political victory would herald for many Dominicans New Yorkers, a waning of interest in, and contact with, island political affairs and politicians. This is not the case, however. Links with the Dominican Republic continue to remain strong and

Dominican immigrants continue to be enriched by their capacity to contribute to, and draw upon, resources in the Dominican Republic as well as the United States.

Consider the character of Guillermo Linares' political campaign. In the month's prior to the election, he proved adept at enlisting support and raising funds in both places.[3] His endorsements from powerful New Yorkers, such as the mayor, were matched by enforcements by prominent island politicians, such as high-ranking officials of the Dominican Liberation Party (PLD). During the break between the primary and general election, Linares returned to the Dominican Republic for a brief stay. There, rallies were held in support of his candidacy which generated funds for his campaign and afforded photo opportunities that were carried in New York newspapers like Listín, USA.

Another, remarkable example of how Dominican ethnic politics encompasses both New York City and the island republic is found in a letter written in Spanish by Linares' mother from her home in the Dominican Republic. In this letter, which was deposited in scores of residential mailboxes throughout Washington Heights, we see a Dominican national urging New Yorkers to vote for her son. The letter's homespun quality and intimate details transport the reader back to a familiar place far removed from New York's "mean streets:"

> As a mother of 9 children and 10 grandchildren, I have had many occasions to be proud in my life. But never have I felt as proud as I do at this moment. Next Thursday, my son Guillermo will have the opportunity to become the first Dominican to serve as a member of the New York City Council.

She goes on to appeal to the sentiments of many Dominican New Yorkers who are far from loved ones, when she writes, "Unfortunately I cannot be there personally on Thursday to share this important moment in Guillermo's life. (I will be in Cabrera, Dominican Republic, from where I am writing you this card.) " But, she reminds them that telephone lines do connect a people divided only by geography, not kinship, sentiment, or national pride.

> I will be waiting for the phone call to hear the good news. Please remember to vote for Guillermo Linares.... You will have a member of the City Council who will make you proud. And you're going to contribute to the phone call from Guillermo to his mother that will be very, very special!

The demand by Dominicans who have become U.S. citizens to retain rights in the Dominican Republic by dint of their Dominican birth is another example of an overall strategy to forge lives aquí and allá. It will be recalled that some 22 percent of all Dominicans in New York City are U.S. citizens (Grasmuck and Pessar, forthcoming). Many of these naturalized Dominicans are critical of the constraints that one-country citizenship places on them. In the past, some have pressured Dominican legislators to consider a proposal for dual-citizenship. More recently, Dominicans have organized across island party lines to support an amendment to the Dominican constitution that would allow persons to reclaim their Dominican citizenship upon permanent return to the Republic. Indeed, the amendment was passed in the Fall of 1994 with the strong endorsement of many Dominican organizations in the United States and the backing of the major Dominican political parties. The existence of this transnational coalition reveals how U.S. citizens of Dominican birth are attempting to maximize their opportunities for political participation and a political voice in both the United States and the Dominican Republic. It also suggests that politicians in the Dominican Republic have realized (like officials in many other labor-exporting nations) that members of their diaspora community are resources that should not and need not be lost to the home country.

The Dominican ethnic economy is another site for the forging of transnational ties between New York and the Dominican Republic. Critics may be right in accusing some Dominican merchants of purveying an "ethnic nostalgia" that promotes transience among Dominican New Yorkers (Torres-Saillant 1989). However, these ethnic entrepreneurs are hardly sentimentalists. By adopting a marketing strategy that refuses to be bound by either nation, they reap sizable material rewards.

Consider the case of Rafael Gómez. The 20-year-old son of a large landholder and coffee merchant, Rafael arrived in New York in 1971. After a few years of working as a cook in a Cuban-owned restaurant, Rafael realized that he could not advance economically by remaining an employee. He was fortunate in having no debts related to his emigration, and had already managed to save several thousands of dollars. Rafael persuaded two of his cousins, who were also residing in New York, to invest with him in the purchase of a *bodega* in Queens. Funding for the venture came not only from these cousins but also from Rafael's father, who sought to diversify and "internationalize" his commercial interests.

Unfortunately, the *bodega* was robbed repeatedly during the 1980s, compelling Rafael to seek a less dangerous line of business. He found it in an apparel factory whose retiring Puerto Rican owner sought a buyer for his business. Since he lacked knowledge of the garment trade, Rafael went into partnership with an uncle who had worked for many years in an apparel shop owned by a Dominican immigrant. Their shop currently employs approximately 50 workers, most of whom are Dominican women. After several years of experience in managing his New York shop and obtaining contracts from U.S. manufacturers, Rafael decided it was time to expand his operations into the Dominican export-processing market. In 1989 he entered into partnership with his father and brother, purchasing a garment factory employing over 200 workers in a Dominican Export Processing Zone (*zona franca*).

When asked whether he plans to remain permanently in the United States or return one day to the Dominican Republic, Rafael, an ordinarily highly decisive man, is equivocal. He states that he is proud to be a U.S. citizen. He chose to naturalize because "I became a man here; I married and have had all my children here. I owe most of my success to opportunities I was given in this country." Yet he goes on to explain that he has built a large home in the Dominican capital and likes "having a business in Santo Domingo, because even though I am a U.S. citizen, you have to be a realist. You never know when things will get really bad for Dominicans [in the U.S].....I like to know that I have a home there, too."

It is not only successful Dominicans like Rafael who continue to retain links with the island. The less successful, too, send remittances back home. For some time now, immigrants' remittances have ranked as the second most important source of foreign exchange in the Dominican Republic, trailing only tourism. And as for tourism, in 1985 Dominican immigrants accounted for one-fifth of the total number of international visitors and almost one-third of the total amount of revenue brought in by tourism (Guarnizo 1992: 327). By 1986, some 60 percent of the formal housing industry on the island had been purchased by Dominicans residing abroad (Guarnizo 1994: 79). If we group remittances with immigrants' participation in the tourist, housing, and other key industries, immigrants emerge as the single most important social group contributing to the Dominican national economy (Ibid: 78-79). These investments not only invigorate the Dominican economy, but also create a psychological and material bridge back "home."

We have focussed here on the social and economic linkages between the Dominican Republic and New York. Such linkages also exist in the arena of popular culture. Consider, for example, the hit song, "Voy pa lla," which was blasted from speakers in *bodegas*, restaurants, and cars in Dominican New York neighborhoods during the summer of 1992. The recording artist, Antony Santos, sings that he is going over there (an unspecified "over there") to find the woman who dominates him in order to bring her back to an unspecified "here." A tremendous hit in both New York and the Dominican Republic, the song employs a familiar formula to evoke male pain and celebrate macho assertiveness (see, Pacini-Hernández 1995). At the same time, it also recognizes that for a Dominican people whose boundaries have become blurred, "over there" and "over here" could be Washington Heights or Santo Domingo—whichever place the listener doesn't happen to be (McLane 1995).

"YOURS IS A COUNTRY FOR WOMEN; OURS IS A COUNTRY FOR MEN"

One of the primary reasons why ties between New York and the Dominican Republic are so strong is that most newcomers arrive with the intention of returning to the island one day. Yet over time, the resolve of many women to return falters. Instead, they come to devise strategies, often against their husband's wishes, to remain in the United States. To appreciate why wives and husbands can find themselves at loggerheads over the issue of settlement versus return, we must reexamine the benefits won and privileges lost by women and men while residing in New York and in the Dominican Republic, respectively.

As we saw in the last chapter, regular employment in New York has allowed many women to negotiate more equitable gender relations within their families. A return to the Dominican Republic means a return to a society where regular employment is less readily available and less socially acceptable for these women who now consider themselves members of the Dominican upper middle class. Indeed, Luis Guarnizo's recent study of returnee families revealed that women were four times more likely than males to be economically dependent either on their spouses or on U.S.-based economic support—such as federal assistance and family remittances (Guarnizo, forthcoming). Women were often called upon to symbolize their family's newly-acquired, upward mobility by confining their work to the domestic sphere (Bueno forthcoming). When returnee women did generate an independent income this was often through activities that remained linked to the home, such as managing a commercial telephone booth located on their property or selling wares out of their homes.

Mindful of the potential loss that return migration poses to their newfound gains, many female Dominican New Yorkers strategize to prolong their family's stay in the United States. Indeed, several of my female informants maximized expenditures on expensive durable goods, such as appliances, furniture, and automobiles. These purchases both contributed to a more comfortable and appealing life in the United

States and reduced the amount of savings available for return to the Dominican Republic.

Dominican men, by contrast, are often heard to comment, "Five dollars wasted today means five more years of postponing the return to the Dominican Republic." Men try to reduce what they spend on commodities and entertainment in the United States in anticipation of a speedy and successful return to the island. Social advancement ranks high among the benefits these men anticipate upon return. Most do, in fact, attain this goal. In his recent study of returnees, Luis Guarnizo (forthcoming) found that the majority were currently proprietors of their own businesses.

As we learned in Chapter 4, Dominican men in New York are deprived of some of the societal resources that traditionally facilitated and "justified" male privilege in the home and community. Dominican men's loss of control over and access to "the streets," a public space conventionally understood to be a male bastion, is a case in point. One male hotel worker lamented, "My life here comes down to a simple round of home to work and then home again." He contrasted this with the spirited hours he had spent with male friends in bars and social clubs in the Dominican Republic prior to emigration. There are certainly similar settings in New York where males can socialize freely. Nonetheless, many are so anxious to repay debts and begin to accumulate savings that they discipline themselves to avoid such places. They also work at jobs that often impose a far more rigid work schedule than was the case in the Dominican Republic. Tardiness due to a hangover and oversleeping may lead to being fired in New York.

Moreover, while Dominicans have put their stamp on certain neighborhood streets in Manhattan, most of these streets remain potentially dangerous and alienating places that men frequently avoid. There is the potential for harassment by and run-ins with the police and agents of the feared Immigration and Naturalization Service. Only recently a Dominican man was choked and suffocated to death by a policeman. The victim had been playing basketball with his family, when he was charged with disturbing the peace and resisting arrest. The streets are also made dangerous by the presence of gangs, muggers, and drug pushers who enforcement agents either cannot or will not remove from the streets. Under such threatening conditions many men have responded by avoiding street life, opting instead to spend far more time in the home, a social space normally associated with women and children.

Dominican men look forward to returning to the Dominican Republic where they will regain those public spaces where men socialize without fear, spend their own discretionary funds, and forge personal and family reputations far beyond the watchful gaze of female kin. As one male returnee told me, "Your country is a country for women; mine is for men. And I am happy to be back because once again it is the man in the street and the woman in the house." His comments stand in stark contrast to those of a female returnee who stated, "I prefer to live in the U.S., because there you can earn your own money, the family is closer, you have control over your husband, you know when he is going out and when he will be back....Men are more human" (Bueno, forthcoming: 6).

For their part, migration to New York has enabled Dominican women to actually enlarge their knowledge of and access to the world beyond the household. They negotiate public thoroughfares and public transport on their way to and from work, their children's schools, and government offices. In this regard, I still recall an awkward, yet telling, scene from the 1980s. After concluding an interview with a Dominican couple in Washington Heights, I pulled out a subway map and explained that I was trying to figure out the best route to a Lower East Side address. The man politely took the map and unsuccessfully puzzled through the intricacies of the New York City transit system. His wife then motioned me to the kitchen. Her frequent job changes and her experiences with several social service agencies scattered throughout the city had necessitated a mastery of the subway lines. While out of her husband's earshot, she easily explained the most appropriate route.

Dominican women say they feel liberated by their their new-found ability to travel widely on their way to and from work and en route to other destinations. "In my country there is always a lot of gossip about women who spend too much time away from their homes. People think the woman is up to no good. Here, there is more understanding that the woman has to leave her home to work and help support the family."

This freedom of mobility unfortunately often recedes once women return to the Dominican Republic. Part of the problem is that there is less tolerance for women's mobility on the island, a situation only reinforced by the lack of socially acceptable transportation facilities at the disposal of upper middle class women. As one returnee explained:

> The greatest difference in the lifestyles of both countries is liberty....Transportation [there] is better; you can buy a car at a reasonable price. Life is easier for women. They can go out, work, find somebody to take care of the children, etc. If you don't have a car, you can take a subway, a bus, a taxi, you don't have to stay in the house. There are many restrictions for women here in the [Dominican Republic] (Bueno, forthcoming: 34-35).

Paradoxically, female returnees, who are usually unemployed and have domestic servants, report that while they have more free time for recreation, there are far fewer options and opportunities for women than in New York. As Carmen recounted:

> I see my husband much less now that we are back. He goes out almost every night with his friends to a club. In New York we used to go out more as a couple, to movies or to a museum. If I go out now, it is with the children to a birthday party or to the pool club.

Although female returnees commonly state that their freedoms as women and wives have diminished upon return, most counter that their satisfaction as mothers has increased. The women are thankful for the greater time they have with children both because the women tend not to be working outside the home and because there are less diversions to draw children away from the family. "As a mother and as a woman I prefer being here with my children. You can be closer to your children and help them with school and friends. You cannot do that in the U.S., because soon after your children start school you are forced to work" (Ibid: 34). Women also contend that the schools in the Dominican Republic are superior to those in the United States, in part because they better enforce discipline and support the parents' rights over those of the children.

A FRAGILE RETURN

Many Dominicans (particularly men) yearn to return. Yet, the actual circumstances of their return and reincorporation are often fraught with disappointment and insecurity. One factor that contributes to dissatisfaction upon return is Dominicans' tendency to idealize "home" when they are abroad. This romanticization of "home," which most immigrants experience, both arises from and fuels unflattering comparisons between the United States and the Dominican Republic. The comparisons may be frivolous: Coca Cola tasted better there. Or they may be quite serious, as when a family huddling around a warm stove in a freezing New York tenement, reminisces about the eternal spring back home. Yet, as Torres-Saillant reminds us, such selective and edenic memories blot out "the high unemployment, the social injustice, the political corruption, the prohibitive cost of living, and the general scarcity which most Dominicans in the island have to endure and which so often drives people to take the most extreme measures in order to escape the homeland" (1989:17).

It is these economic and political problems that Dominicans reencounter when they return. Some returnees are able to reestablish themselves securely back home; others find it a struggle. Returnees who reinsert themselves in an innovative niche within the Dominican economy are likely to experience most successful reentry. The del Castillo family returned in 1978 after having lived in New York for 11 years. At the time of their departure, Pedro was employed as a building superintendent and Ramona worked as a hospital orderly. The couple and their four children moved into the home in Santiago which they had built while in New York. In anticipation of a return, Pedro had made several trips to the island to consult with family and friends regarding potential business ventures. He became convinced of the need for modern photocopying facilities and used the couple's savings to purchase and ship several machines from the United States to the Dominican Republic. Over the years the del Castillos have opened three additional stores and have also expanded to provide a repair service for commercial photocopying equipment.

Returnees who invest in economic activities that have long been saturated by earlier returnees tend not to fare as well. In the context of a relatively small and inelastic local market for consumer goods and services, returnees frequently flounder when investing in such redundant operations as money-exchanges, small supermarkets, and gas stations. This is the problem faced by the Lara family, who returned to Santo Domingo in 1985 after seven years in New York. The family spent over a year living off their savings before they began a modest money-exchange and credit business out of their home. Unlike the del Castillos, the Laras returned without much planning. Their return was precipitated by an injury Alberto Lara sustained at work. As an undocumented immigrant, he was fearful of applying for work compensation benefits, yet was too infirm to return to his previous job. Injured and disillusioned, Alberto convinced his wife to return home where he could recuperate and invest their savings in a business.

I learned the Lara family's history from Mrs. Lara, whom I met some years ago in New York. She explained that in order to afford their home in Santo Domingo and sustain a middle-class life style there, she has to spend half of every year in New York City where she works in a garment factory owned by a Dominican friend. "While it is hard to leave my children behind, this is the only way that we can afford to send them to private schools and allow them to keep up with their friends whose parents come from monied backgrounds. Without a lot of savings and contacts, modest people like us can't make it back home."

The Lara family's story is not unusual. In the early 1980s when I conducted research in return migrant neighborhoods in Santiago, I found that most of the households were unable to meet their consumption needs through locally generated income. Nearly two-thirds of the households interviewed obtained all or the majority of their income from sources in the United States. These sources included savings, child support, alimony, and salaries acquired through temporary U.S. employment. Indeed, almost one-fourth of the households surveyed participated in this type of circulating migration (Grasmuck and Pessar 1991: 86-87).

If returnees encounter harsh economic circumstances when they go back, they also often find that they do not receive the warm welcome home from their compatriots that they anticipated. In the early 1980s when I began my research in the Dominican Republic, I often heard snide comments about *retornados* from nonmigrant middle-class and upper-class Dominicans. *Retornados* were commonly depicted as country bumpkins who had returned to Dominican cities from a stint in Manhattan, but had yet to shed their peasant naivete and lifeways. One deprecating joke involved a returnee who turned on his radio in Santo Domingo immediately after getting off the plane. "Look," he said to his wife. "These *gringo* radios are pretty smart. This one already has learned Spanish and we've just arrived." Despite the sarcasm, however, there was still a general consensus then that returnees were hard-working folk who had sacrificed abroad to better their lot at home.

More recently, the image on the island of Dominican immigrants and *retornados* has turned far more alien and sinister. Back in the '80s Dominican immigrants were fondly called *dominicanos ausentes* (absent Dominicans), an acknowledgment of the fact that, while they might temporarily be residing abroad, they still very much belonged within the national fold. Today's more popular terms—"domínican" (rather than the more authentically-Spanish, "dominicano"), "dominicanyork" (the antithesis of an authentic Dominican), and *cadenú* (a gold necklace wearer, an allusion to drug kingpins and pushers)—serve to highlight the social distance that many island Dominicans seek to impose between themselves and Dominican immigrants and returnees.

Overt discrimination is also common, with the result that returnees are frequently barred from prestigious business associations, private social clubs, and private schools. Luis Guarnizo observes: "When looking for housing, it is now customary for nonmigrant middle-class families to ask, as a matter of course, whether there are *retornados* or *domínicans* living in the area—or building—they are considering to move into. If so, no further consideration would be needed for withdrawing their bid" (Ibid:37). It is not surprising, therefore, that one-third of the 150 returnees surveyed by Guarnizo in 1991 reported that they wanted to reemigrate to the United States. Indeed, over one half of these individuals hoped to leave within a year's time (Guarnizo, forthcoming: 20).

CHALLENGES THAT LIE AHEAD

The Dominican diaspora in the United States and the Dominican Republic has been frequently misunderstood and maligned by members of the dominant society on both shores. The media coverage of Dominicans in the New York City English-language press, for example, has been minimal, despite the fact that Dominicans are the largest immigrant group in the metropolitan area. Those articles that have appeared have tended to dwell on incidents of drug-dealing and crime (Duany 1994). One particularly egregious article published recently in the *New York Post* with a dateline from San Francisco de Macoris, Dominican Republic states:

> The Dominican Republic has always exported talent to the United States. The sports pages are filled with the statistics of Dominican baseball heroes in the Major Leagues. But for every George Bell...thrilling American audiences, there are now a dozen lethal drug dealers from San Francisco de Macoris terrorizing neighborhoods in upper Manhattan... "We are the Dominican-Yorks", they all chuckle, "and we are getting away with murder on the streets of New York" (McAlary 1992:3).

Clearly there is a need to confront and contest this pernicious characterization of Dominicans. Some Dominican New Yorkers have taken up this challenge. In the editorial section of another New York daily, Silvio Torres-Saillant sought to educate New Yorkers about the Dominicans in their midst and to explain why Dominican New Yorkers are so troubled by "ethnic antipathy". He concludes his piece by stating:

> Immigration is irreversible. What follows now is the journey toward (Dominican-) Americanness, which means that now comes the struggle for space in a new country and the fight to ward off vilification. A significant aspect of this fight takes place at the level of discourse. It is the lot of the marginal to have to live hyperconsciously (1993:64).

Dominican leaders are aware that their community's limited power and economic resources are stumbling blocks in the battle over symbolic representation. Change will come, for example, when Dominican New Yorkers have enough economic clout to refuse to advertise in, and subscribe to, those newspapers which persist in publishing denigrating pieces about the Dominican community.

Yet, Dominicans in New York face an uncertain economic future. They hold a disadvantaged position within New York's ethnic hierarchy; and as anthropologist Jorge Duany observes, under these circumstances, Dominicans' "'assimilation' may not be to mainstream values and expectations, but to the adversarial stance of impoverished groups relegated to the bottom of the new economic hourglass" (1994: 44).[4] Whether Dominicans in New York will be successful in unifying as a community to make common cause with other disadvantaged minorities, like Puerto Ricans and African Americans, remains to be seen.

In this study I have referred repeatedly to the Dominican "community." If Dominican New Yorkers follow the pattern of earlier ethnic groups, they are likely to identify as members of a distinct community as long as they are targeted for discrimination and treated by members of the majority society as an undifferentiated mass. Yet, as I have noted repeatedly here, Dominicans are internally segmented and stratified along class, gender, generational, and to a lesser extent, racial lines. There is reason to question whether, for example, a Dominican who has accumulated substantial wealth in both the United States and the Dominican Republic and owns comfortable private homes in both places will identify and feel solidarity with a poverty-stricken, Dominican female head of household in Washington Heights. Or as one Dominican New Yorker, put it more colorfully, "We may claim that Oscar de la Renta (a famous Dominican fashion designer) is part of the community, but I very much doubt he would make the same claim."

The Dominican community in New York now embraces new arrivals as well as second- and third-generation Dominican New Yorkers. The identity problems generated by this mixture of "old" and "new" were nicely captured in the autobiographical writings of a second-generation Dominican enrolled in one of my university classes.

> Throughout school the majority of my classmates and friends were white. As more Latinos, specifically Dominicans, arrived to my home town [in Long Island, New York] I felt that, just having "come off the boat," they seemed very different than me, an American with a Dominican background. My eighth grade industrial arts class is a perfect example. I was asked by the teacher to sit with three Dominican students who spoke very little English. Every day we all sat at a table and [with me] acting as the translator, we would work our way through the day's lesson. The teacher felt that I was the perfect person to help them with the work. In reality I felt ostracized and punished. I recognized that I was Dominican and spoke Spanish but why should I be punished for that! The problem was I was being grouped with these students.

Dominicans in the other branch of the diaspora, comprised of returnees and circular migrants, also struggle with problems of identity and community. Many Dominican New Yorkers emphasize their Dominicanness while in New York. As one young Dominican woman put it, "Dominicans in New York want to be more Dominican than the Dominicans back home." Yet, when they do return home, many are perceived by nonmigrants as Americanized Dominicans whose behavior is an affront to "authentic" Dominican culture. Moreover, Many returnees have been unable to gain access to the networks and social circles in the Dominican Republic that their newfound wealth "should" afford them (Guarnizo 1994). Some returnees, like their counterparts in New York, are responding to this discrimination by banding together to form self-help associations such as business and cultural associations. Returnees, however, have yet to join together as a political constituency to demand a more respected and guiding role in contemporary Dominican society. In this regard, *retornados* would do well to begin by affirming their own sizeable contributions to the "economic democratization" of the island. As one returnee observes:

> Migrants show off their power and their wealth precisely because most Dominicans don't have either of them. Instead of diminishing, discrimination enhances migrants' self-esteem. The *tradicionales* (traditional bourgeoisie) criticize their sumptuous consumption, but that consumption generates development, creates more business" (Guarnizo 1994: 81-82).

Many of the people described in this book are creatively and effectively forging transnational identities, social relations, economic opportunities, political participation, and popular culture. As transnational actors, they are contributing to the new globalizing trends that mark to our contemporary world. They are, nonetheless, trend setters, who must confront skepticism, if not hostility, from those who insist that immigrants must settle permanently and assimilate totally in the United States, and that returnees must cheerfully accept the status quo of the society they have temporarily abandoned. One of the challenges Dominicans and other contemporary "transmigrants" face is convincing governments to facilitate rather than impede the operation of transnational flows. The recent amendment to the Dominican constitution permitting individuals who have chosen to naturalize in the United States to reclaim their Dominican citizenship at a later date is a step in the right direction. Another challenge Dominicans confront is to reassure "traditionalists" in both countries that some of the new hybrid identities and cultural products of this transnational encounter—for example, "Dominicanyorks," Dominican "Spanglish" (Spanish and English), and the current blend of merengue and "hip hop"—are vibrant and enriching additions to both societies.

The challenges the Dominican diaspora community faces are great. So is the determination of many Dominican New Yorkers and *retornados* to succeed. As Euclid Mejía, the first Dominican principal of George Washington High School, told his audience on the occasion of Dominican Independence Day:

> I come from a small island in the Caribbean that had to fight the major powers of the day, the French and the Spaniards, and then, for 22 years, the Haitians. I sense that fighting spirit in the Dominican community here. It's in our national anthem: We'll keep fighting, we'll keep coming back, and we'll win" (*New York Newsday* 1994: 15).

END NOTES

1. Works by Dominicans, which have been written in, or translated into, English, are giving Dominicans a voice within the larger North American society. Some of these works include: Julia Alvarez's *Homecoming* (Grove Press, 1994), *How the García Girls Lost Their Accents* (Algonquin, 1990), *In the Time of the Butterflies* (Algonquin, 1994), and *The Other Side* (Penguin, 1995); island poet, Pedro Mir's *Countersong to Walt Whitman and Other Poems* (Azul Edi-

tions, 1993); Aída Cartagena Portalatín's epic poem, *Yanta Tierra* (Azul Editions, 1995); Frank Moya Pons' *The Dominican Republic: A National History* (Hispaniola Books, 1995), and a Dominican research monograph series published by the City University of New York's Dominican Studies Institute.

2. This section on Dominican politics draws heavily on information generously provided by political scientist Pamela Graham, who is currently completing a dissertation at the University of Chapel Hill, North Carolina on Dominican immigration and transnational politics.

3. I have examined the political campaign of Guillermo Linares, not to showcase his political career, but because his compaign effectively illustrates how Dominican politics in New York sometimes incorporates transnational ties, resources, and identities.

4. .In the original, Duany actually quotes Alejandro Portes and Min Zhou (1993) who have introduced this notion of a segmented, rather than homogeneous and uniform, assimilation for new immigrants.

References

Báez, Clara and Ginny Taulé
1993 "Posición socio-cultural y económica de la mujer en la república dominicana." Género 1(2): 1-144.

Basch, Linda, Nina Glick Schiller, and Cristina Szanton-Blanc
1994 Nations Unbound: Transnationalized Projects and the Deterritorialized Nation-State. New York: Gordon and Breach.

Bragg, Rick
1994 "New York's Bodegas Become Islands Under Seige." The New York Times, March 20, pp. B1, B39.

Brown, Susan E.
1975 "Love Unites Them and Hunger Separates Them: Poor Women in the Dominican Republic. In Rayna Reiter, ed., Toward an Anthropology of Women. New York: Monthly Review Press.

Bueno, Lourdes
forthcoming "Dominican Women's Experiences of Return Migration: The Life Stories of Five Women." In Patricia R. Pessar, ed., Caribbean Circuits: Emigration, Remittances and Return. New York: Center for Migration Studies.

Carter, Sakinah
1994 "Shades of Identity: Puerto Ricans and Dominicans Across Racial Paradigms," Senior Essay, Latin American Studies, Yale University.

Castro, Max
1985 "Dominican Journey: Patterns, Context, and Consequences of Migration From the Dominican Republic to the United States." Ph.D. dissertation, University of North Carolina, Chapel Hill.

Coco De Filippis, Daisy and Franklin Gutiérrez
1994 Historia De Washington Heights Y Otros Ricones Del Mundo/ Stories From Washington Heights and Other Corners of the World. New York: Latino Press.

del Castillo José and Martin F. Murphy
  1987   "Migration, National Identity, and Cultural Policy." The Journal of Ethnic Studies: 15(3): 49-69.

Duany, Jorge
  1994   Quisqueya on the Hudson: The Transnational Identity of Dominicans in Washington Heights. New York: Dominican Research Monographs, The CUNY Dominican Studies Institute.

Feathersone, Mike
  1990   Global Culture. London: Sage Publications.

Fix, Michael and Jeffrey Passel
  1994   Immigration and Immigrants. Washington, D.C.: The Urban Institute.

Garrison, Vivian and Carol I. Weiss
  1979   "Dominican Family Networks and the United States Immigration Policy: A Case Study." International Migration Review 12(2): 264- 283.

Georges, Eugenia
  1990   The Making of a Transnational Community: Migration, Development, and Cultural Change in the Dominican Republic. New York: Columbia University Press.

  1988   "Dominican Self-Help Associations in Washington Heights: Integration of a New Population in a Multiethnic Neighborhood." New Directions for Latino Public Policy Research, Working Paper No. 1, Inter- University Program for Latino Research and the Social Science Research Council.

  1987   "A Comment on Dominican Ethnic Associations." In Constance Sutton and Elsa Chaney, eds., Caribbean Life in New York City: Sociocultural Dimensions. New York: Center for Migration Studies.

  1984   "New Immigrants and the Political Process: Dominicans in New York." Occasional Paper 45, Center for Latin American and Caribbean Studies, New York University.

Gilbertson, Greta
  1995   "Problems Confronting Latino Communities in New York City." Unpublished (draft) report (Fordham University).

Gilbertson, Greta and Douglas Gurak
  1993   "Broadening the Enclave Debate: The Labor Market Experiences of Dominican and Colombian Men in New York City." Sociological Forum 8(2): 205-220.

  1992   "Household Transitions in the Migrations of Dominicans and Colombians to New York." International Migration Review 26(1): 22-45.

González, David
  1992 "Dominican Immigration Alters Hispanic New York." New York Times, September 1, pg. A1.
  1993 "Unmasking Roots of Washington Heights Violence." New York Times, October 21, pg. B1.

Goris-Rosario, Anneris Altagracia
  1994 "The Role of the Ethnic Community and the Workplace in the Integration of Immigrants: A Case Study of Dominicans in New York City" Ph.D. dissertation, Fordham University, New York.

Grasmuck, Sherri and Patricia R.Pessar
  forthcoming "First and Second Generation Settlement of Dominicans in the United States: 1960-1990." In Silvia Pedraza and Rubén Rumbaut, eds., Origins and Destinies: Immigration, Race, and Ethnicity in America, Belmont, CA.: Wadsworth Press.
  1991 Between Two Islands: Dominican International Migration. Berkeley: University of California Press.

Guarnizo, Luis Eduardo
  forthcoming "Going Home: Class, Gender, and Household Transformation Among Dominican Return Migrants." In Patricia R. Pessar, ed., Caribbean Circuits: Emigration, Remittances, and Return. New York: Center for Migration Studies.
  1994 "Los Dominicanyorks: The Making of a Binational Society." ANNALS 553: 70-86.
  1992 "One Country in Two: Dominican Owned Firms in New York and in the Dominican Republic." Ph.D. dissertation, The Johns Hopkins University, Baltimore, Maryland.

Gurak, Douglas and Mary Kritz
  1987 "Family Formation and Marital Selection Among Colombian and Dominican Immigrants in New York City." International Migration Review 21(2): 275-298.
  1982 "Dominican and Colombian Women in New York City: Migration Structure and Employment Patterns." Migration Today 10(3-4): 14-21.

Hendricks, Glenn
  1974 The Dominican Diaspora: From the Dominican Republic to New York City--Villagers in Transition. New York: Teachers College Press.

Hernández, Julio and Fernando Lescaille
  1991 "A Proposal for a Dominican-Based District in Washington Heights and Inwood," Presented by The North Manhattan Committee for Fair Representation.

Hernández, Ramona, Francisco Rivera-Batiz, and Roberto Agodini
  1995 Dominican New Yorkers: A Socioeconomic Profile, 1990. New York: Dominican Research Monographs, The CUNY Dominican Studies Institute.

Hood, Jane C.
  1983 Becoming a Two-Job Family: Role Bargaining in Dual Worker Households. New York: Praeger.

Lamphere, Louise, Patricia Zavella, and Felipe Gonzales with Peter Evans
  1993 Sunbelt Working Mothers. Ithaca, New York: Cornell University Press.

Linares, Guillermo
  1989 "Dominicans in New York: Superando los Obstaculos y Aquiriendo Poder; The Struggle for Community Control in District 6," Centro Bulletin, 2(5): 77-84.

Lowenstein, Steven
  1989 Frankfort on the Hudson: The German-Jewish Community of Washington Heights, 1933-1983. Detroit: Wayne State University.

Marshall, Adriana
  1983 "Immigration in a Surplus-Worker Labor Market: The Case of New York." Occasional Paper 39, Center for Latin American and Caribbean Studies, New York University.

Martin, John
  1966 Overtaken by Events: From the Death of Trujillo to the Civil War. New York: Doubleday.

McAlary, Mike
  1992 "Washington Hts.' Deadly Dominican Connection." New York Post, September 16, pp. 3, 13.

McLane, Daisann
  1995 "Islands of Stylin...Dominican Maleness and Popular Music in Washington Heights." Paper presented at the conference, "Beyond a Boundary: Black Male Culture in New York," New York University (February).

Mitchell, Christopher
  1992 Western Hemisphere Immigration and United States Foreign Policy. University Park, Pennsylvania: The Pennsylvania State University Press.

Myerson, Allen R.
  1992 "Dominicans Thrive Where Big Chains Won't Go." The New York Times, January 7, pp. C1, C3.

New York Newsday
  1994 "Winning Spirit." March 7, p. 15.

Pacini-Hernández, Deborah
  1995 Bachata: A Social History of Dominican Popular Music. Philadelphia: Temple University Press.

Pessar, Patricia R.
1994   "Sweatshop Workers and Domestic Ideologies: Dominican Women in New York's Apparel Industry." International Journal of Urban and Regional Research 18(1): 127-142.

1984   "The Linkage Between the Household and the Workplace in the Experience of Dominican Immigrant Women in the United States." International Migration Review 18(4): 1188-1211.

Portes, Alejandro and Min Zhou
1991   "The Second Generation: Segmented Assimilation and Its Variants Among Post-1965 Immigrant Youth." Working Paper 34, Rusell Sage Foundation, New York.

Rosenbaum, Emily and Greta Gilbertson
1995   "Mother's Labor Force Participation in New York City: A Reappraisal of the Influence of Household Extension." Journal of Marriage and the Family 57: 243-249.

Sassen, Saskia
1991   The Global City: New York, London, Tokyo. Princeton: Princeton University Press.

Torres-Saillant, Silvio
1993   "Dominicans and the U.S. Go Way, Way Back." New York Newsday. June 28, 1993, p. 64.

1989   "Dominicans as a New York Community: A Social Appraisal." Punto 7 Review: A Journal of Marginal Discourse 2(1): 7-25.

U.S. Department of Commerce, Bureau of the Census 1990
1990   Census Special Tabulations, Persons of Hispanic Origin for the United States.

U.S. Immigration and Naturalization Service
1990   Annual Report of the Immigration and Naturalization Service. Washington, D.C.: U.S. Government Printing Office.

Waldinger, Roger
1987   "Changing Ladders and Musical Chairs: Ethnicity and Opportunity in Post-Industrial New York." Politics and Society 15(4): 369-402.

1986   Through the Eye of the Needle: Immigrants and Enterprise in New York's Garment Trade. New York: New York University Press.

Warren, Robert
1992   "Estimates of the Unauthorized Immigrant Population Residing in the U.S. by Country of Origin and State of Residence." Washington, D.C.: Statistics Bureau, Immigration and Naturalization Service.

1988   "Legalization Data and Other Statistical Information About Dominican Migration to the United States." Paper presented at the Conference on Dominican Migration, Fundación Friedrich Ebert, Santo Domingo, Dominican Republic.

Williams, Terry
   1989   The Cocaine Kids. New York: Addison-Wesley Publishing, Inc.